Guidelines and Recommended Practices for the Individualized Family Service Plan

Second Edition
April 1991

EDITED BY:

Mary J. McGonigel

Roxane K. Kaufmann

Beverley H. Johnson

CONTRIBUTORS:

Donald B. Bailey

Carl J. Dunst

Joicey L. Hurth

Shirley Kramer

Ann P. Turnbull

And the IFSP Task Force
(See pages xi-xii for a complete list of parent and professional participants.)

Association for the Care of Children's Health
Bethesda, Maryland

Guidelines and Recommended Practices for the Individualized Family Service Plan
Second Edition, First Printing
April 1991

ISBN 0-937821-77-2

Association for the Care of Children's Health
7910 Woodmont Avenue, Suite 300
Bethesda, MD 20814

Sample citation:

McGonigel, M. J., & Johnson, B. H. (1991). An overview. In M. J. McGonigel, R. K. Kaufmann, & B. H. Johnson (Eds.), *Guidelines and Recommended Practices for the Individualized Family Service Plan* (2nd ed.) (pp. 1-5). Bethesda, MD: Association for the Care of Children's Health.

Additional copies may be purchased from:

Association for the Care of Children's Health
7910 Woodmont Avenue, Suite 300
Bethesda, MD 20814

Table of Contents

Appendices

Acknowledgments

Four years ago, when I was asked to serve, on behalf of the Association for the Care of Children's Health, as the Lead of the NEC*TAS Expert Team for the IFSP, I saw an exciting opportunity to expand our work in family-centered care. Although all members of the Team realized the critical importance of the IFSP to successful implementation of P.L. 99-457, no one fully realized the scope of the work we were proposing or the complexity of our task. The resulting document, *Guidelines and Recommended Practices for the Individualized Family Service Plan*, was published two years ago.

Many people participated in the development of that publication -- people representing federal and state agencies, various organizations, and early intervention programs; professionals from many disciplines; and parents caring for children with special needs.

Don Bailey, Carl Dunst, Shirley Kramer, and Ann Turnbull, all members of the IFSP Expert Team, made thoughtful and substantive contributions the publication and generously shared time and expertise. The work of the Task Force on the IFSP was critical to the early development of the document and again in reviewing a first draft. Carole Brown, then at OSEP, and Joicey Hurth and Roxane Kaufmann of NEC*TAS were active in planning the development of the document and in bringing together the diverse and talented Expert Team and Task Force.

Co-editors Mary McGonigel, Roxane Kaufmann, and I especially thank Corinne Garland, Nancy DiVenere, Linda Kjerland, and Terri Shelton, each a Task Force member, for the energy, enthusiasm, and expertise with which they responded to our many additional requests for help as we wrestled with the first edition.

We also thank Joyce Lindgren, Polly Edmunds, and Paula Goldberg of the PACER Center and George Jesien of the University of Wisconsin - Madison for their significant contributions to the review process. Ibby Jeppson, Josie Thomas, and Nancy Guadagno, ACCH staff members, also made important contributions to the content and format of the publication. Susan Hom, formerly of NEC*TAS at the Georgetown University Child Development Center, deserved a special acknowledgment for her important work on the Appendices.

Since the book was published in 1989, it has been widely distributed throughout the country to professionals and families working to implement the IFSP component of Part H. The success of that first edition prompted NEC*TAS and ACCH to develop a second edition -- revised and updated to reflect the final regulations related to the IFSP and our growing understanding of best practices for family-centered early intervention.

For the most part, the same people who were so instrumental in developing the first edition were responsible for this new edition. We do want to thank, however, David Jones, of the WINGS Project at the University of Wisconsin - Madison, for his substantial contributions to the new edition, both as a contributor and reviewer; Marcia Decker, of NEC*TAS, for her review of the second edition; and Bobbi Hitt, of ACCH, for her help in updating many of the Appendices.

It has been our privilege to work with NEC*TAS, especially Pat Trohanis, Joicey Hurth, and Joan Danaher, and to be part of their efforts to develop technical assistance for the IFSP component of Part H.

When we began this project in 1987, our hope was that it would result in a document that would help policy makers, planners, providers, and families implement the IFSP component in ways that are consistent with best practices as we understood them then. Writing in her former role as the chairperson of the Federal Interagency Coordinating Council, Madeline Will expressed this same hope -- her letter that appeared in the first edition of *Guidelines and Recommended Practices for the Individualized Family Service Plan* follows these acknowledgements.

My fervent hope today continues to be that each reader of these guidelines will help to shape the best practices of tomorrow for family-centered early intervention.

Beverley H. Johnson
April 1991

UNITED STATES DEPARTMENT OF EDUCATION

OFFICE OF THE ASSISTANT SECRETARY
FOR SPECIAL EDUCATION AND REHABILITATIVE SERVICES

We are presently in the midst of implementing the Part H Early Intervention Program for Handicapped Infants and Toddlers (Public Law 99-457, Education of the Handicapped Act Amendments of 1986). As we rapidly move forward to 1991, the end of the five-year phase-in period that Congress initiated in 1986 to develop comprehensive statewide systems of early intervention services, States must develop policies to put the fourteen required components of Part H into effect. The Individualized Family Service Plan (IFSP), one of these required components, represents the cornerstone of the entire system of early intervention services. The IFSP offers parents and professionals a mechanism to plan coordinated and individualized services to support the development of an infant with special needs in the context of the child's family.

Part H of Public Law 99-457 has given us a significant opportunity to rethink and reconcile what we know about child development with our beliefs about the best ways to provide early intervention services to infants and toddlers with handicaps and their families. Knowing that infants can thrive best in nurturing environments, it is insufficient to be solely child-centered in our approach to early intervention. Our target for service delivery must therefore be the *family*, to enhance the capacity of the family to meet the special needs of the child.

Recognizing the challenge that the IFSP presents, the Office of Special Education and Rehabilitative Services (OSERS) has sponsored several activities to develop viable models for carrying out IFSP's. These activities are particularly timely and important because the IFSP, as an essential component of the Part H early intervention program, must be in place soon -- by the fourth year of a State's participation, all children served under P.L. 99-457 must have an IFSP. We have had continuing support from the Federal Interagency Coordinating Council in implementing these activities. In particular, the Bureau of Maternal and Child Health and Resources Development has collaborated extensively throughout this effort to develop best practices for the IFSP.

A call to the field for best practices in IFSP development was initiated in the fall of 1987, and submissions were analyzed by the Carolina Institute for Research on Infant Personnel Preparation. Based upon the preliminary analysis of the call to the field, an interagency group representing the Office of Special Education Programs, (OSEP), the Bureau of Maternal and Child Health and Resources Development (MCH), and the Early Intervention Consortium funded by the Administration on Developmental Disabilities (ADD) recommended that work to develop best practices be continued. This interagency group became the IFSP Task Force and was expanded to include representatives from the National Institute on Disability and Rehabilitation Research (NIDRR), the National Institute of Mental Health (NIMH), the Administration for Children, Youth and Families (ACYF), parents of children with special needs, and a multidisciplinary group of professionals with expertise in early intervention.

Meeting in May, 1988 the IFSP Task Force began the process that resulted in recommended best practices for IFSP development in the following specific areas: philosophy and conceptual framework, building positive relationships between professionals and families, identifying child and family strengths and needs, developing outcomes, and implementation. This document was written by the subgroup leaders of the Task Force, the NEC*TAS Expert Team, and is based upon the findings of the Task Force and feedback from State representatives.

We are pleased to share with you the product of these activities to develop best practices for the IFSP -- *Guidelines and Recommended Practices for the Individualized Family Service Plan.* We share this with you in the knowledge that the process matters as much as the product -- and that you in your role as parent, professional, or policy planner are critically important in the development of best practices for the IFSP. Read, reflect, and discuss with others the principles in this document. We look forward to continued refinement of these concepts as comprehensive early intervention services become a reality for all children with special needs and their families in this country.

Madeleine Will

Madeleine Will
Assistant Secretary
Chair, Federal Interagency Coordinating Council

Task Force on the IFSP
(Office of Special Education Programs)

NEC*TAS Expert Team

Beverley Johnson, Expert Team Leader, Executive Director, Association for the Care of Children's Health, Bethesda, Maryland.

Mary McGonigel, Associate Director, National Center for Family-Centered Care, Association for the Care of Children's Health.

Donald Bailey, Director of Early Childhood Research, Frank Porter Graham Child Development Center, University of North Carolina at Chapel Hill.

Carl Dunst, Director, Family, Infant and Preschool Program and Center for Family Studies, Western Carolina Center, Morganton, North Carolina.

Shirley Kramer, parent of twins with special needs; Associate Consultant, Project Dakota, Eagan, Minnesota; Chairperson of the Family Subcommittee, Federal ICC.

Ann Turnbull, Co-director, Beach Center on Families and Disability; Professor, Department of Special Education, University of Kansas at Lawrence.

Roxane Kaufmann, Associate Director, NEC*TAS at Georgetown University Child Development Center, Washington, D.C.

Joicey Hurth, Associate Director, NEC*TAS, University of North Carolina at Chapel Hill.

Carole Brown, formerly Education Program Specialist, Office of Special Education Programs, U.S. Department of Education; currently Assistant Professor, Department of Teacher Preparation and Special Education, George Washington University, Washington, D.C.

Task Force
(May 1988 - March 1989)

May Aaronson, Child and Family Support Branch, National Institute of Mental Health.

Kathleen Kirk Bishop, Bureau of Maternal and Child Health and Resources Development, U.S. Department of Health and Human Services.

Edward Bordley, Attorney, parent of an infant with special needs.

Martha Bryan, Office of Special Education Programs, U.S. Department of Education.

David Buckholz, parent of a preschooler with special needs, member of the Maryland ICC.

Karen Buckholz, parent of a preschooler with special needs, Pasadena, Maryland.

Philippa Campbell, Director, Family Child Learning Center, Tallmadge, Ohio.

Roberta Clark, Department of Pediatrics, Howard University Hospital, Washington, D.C.

Jane DeWeerd, Head Start, Administration for Children, Youth, and Families, U.S. Department of Health and Human Services.

Nancy DiVenere, Director, Parents-Helping-Parents of Vermont, Inc., parent of a child with special needs.

Susan Fowler, Associate Professor, University of Kansas at Lawrence.

Corinne Garland, Executive Director, Child Development Resources, Lightfoot, Virginia.

Martha Gilgen, Attorney, Idaho Parents United, Inc., in Boise, parent of a child with special needs.

Josie Gittler, Co-director, National MCH Resource Center, College of Law, University of Iowa, Iowa City.

Alfred Healy, Director, University Affiliated Program, University of Iowa, Iowa City.

Regina Hicks, Coordinator, Child and Adolescent Services, Texas Department of Mental Health and Mental Retardation, Austin, Texas.

Naomi Karp, National Institute on Disability and Rehabilitation Research.

Judith Katz-Levy, Assistant Chief, Child and Family Support Branch, National Institute of Mental Health.

Ted Maloney, Project Director, University of Montana, Missoula.

Jeanne Mendoza, Coordinator, Parents and Professionals Advocating Collaborative Training, San Diego State University.

Dee Moore, parent of an infant who had special needs in Grafton, Virginia, board member of Child Development Resources.

Jennifer Olsen, Project Director, Outreach to Infants in Rural Settings, Idaho University, Moscow.

Patricia Place, NEC*TAS, National Association of State Directors of Special Education, Washington, D.C.

Vicky Rab, Project Coordinator, Project I-TIP, George Washington University, Washington, D.C.

Karme Raggio, parent of a young child with special needs, Washington, D.C.

Ruth Ann Rasbold, NEC*TAS, Federation for Children With Special Needs, Boston, Massachusetts, parent of a child with special needs.

Claire Rudolph, Professor, School of Social Work, Syracuse University, Syracuse, New York.

Hector Sanchez, Head Start, Administration for Children, Youth, and Families, U.S. Department of Health and Human Services.

Terri Shelton, Assistant Professor, Department of Psychiatry, University of Massachusetts Medical Center, Worcester.

Rune Simeonsson, Associate Professor, Frank Porter Graham Child Development Center, University of North Carolina at Chapel Hill.

Meave Stevens-Dominguez, Project Director, Family-Centered Inservice Training Model and Infant Curriculum, University of New Mexico, Albuquerque.

Kathleen Stremel-Campbell, Associate Professor, Special Education Department, University of Southern Mississippi, Hattiesburg.

Jean Ann Summers, Director, Kansas University Affiliated Program, University of Kansas.

Daphne Thomas, Frank Porter Graham Child Development Center, University of North Carolina at Chapel Hill.

Robin Thomas, Director, Child and Family Support Program, Children's Hospital of Seattle and University of Washington at Seattle.

Eva Thorp, Assistant Professor, Special Education Department, University of Illinois, Champaign.

Representatives from ten states attended a technical assistance event in conjunction with the IFSP Task Force meeting. Their comments and suggestions were incorporated in the document.

An Overview

By Mary J. McGonigel and Beverley H. Johnson

Introduction

Public Law 99-457, the Education of the Handicapped Act Amendments of 1986, Part H, directed states "to develop and implement a statewide, comprehensive, coordinated, multidisciplinary, interagency program of early intervention services for handicapped infants and toddlers and their families" {20 USC 671(b)}. As state policy makers, practitioners, and families work together to develop this comprehensive system, they have a unique opportunity to reshape and redirect early intervention services to infants and toddlers with special needs and their families -- to form a "community of caring" (DiVenere, 1988).

Since the first edition of this monograph, the 101st Congress again reauthorized the Education of the Handicapped Act (EHA). This legislation, Public Law 101-476, changed the name of EHA to Individuals with Disabilities Education Act (IDEA) and changed all terminology to *people first* language. The term "handicap" is replaced with "disability." Therefore, "handicapped infants and toddlers" in Part H became "infants and toddlers with disabilities."

In 1986, when Part H was first enacted, perhaps no provision generated more discussion than the requirement for an Individualized Family Service Plan (IFSP). The IFSP is just one component of a statewide system of comprehensive early intervention. The purpose of the IFSP is for families and professionals to work together as a team to identify and mobilize formal and informal resources to help families' reach their chosen goals. The IFSP is a promise to children and families -- a promise that their strengths will be recognized and built on, that their beliefs and values will be respected, that their choices will be honored, and that their hopes and aspirations will be encouraged and enabled.

The IFSP -- the written product itself -- is possibly the least important aspect of the entire IFSP process. Far more important are the interaction, collaboration, and partnerships between families and professionals that are necessary to develop and implement the IFSP. The Parents as Partners Project (1988) at Alta Mira Specialized Family Services, Inc., in Albuquerque, New Mexico, beautifully illustrated this point in their document for other parents, *Preparing for the Individualized Family Service Plan*:

> As you begin this early intervention program you will be asked to form a partnership with the professionals who will be working with your child and family. As with all good relationships, it takes time to build the trust, respect, and sharing that is the foundation of a successful partnership. To this end the Individualized Family Service Plan (IFSP) is not just paperwork or evaluations that must be done so that your child can be enrolled in a program. The IFSP is a partnership that will last the entire time your child and family are with the early intervention program. (p. 1)

The IFSP requires new approaches and practices on the part of the many agencies, institutions, and professional disciplines that provide early intervention services to children with special needs and their families. If the IFSP is to fulfill its promise of meeting the broad-based needs of these children and their families, the same coordination that is

Timetable for Implementation of the IFSP Component

The IFSP provision must be implemented no later than the beginning of the fourth year of the State's participation under Part H. {20 USC 1475}

modeled by the Interagency Coordinating Councils at the state level must become a reality at the local level.

As a field, "early intervention is still in the process of defining itself" (Healy, Keesee, & Smith, 1989, p. 121). Some professionals who provide services to young children with special needs think of themselves first as early intervention practitioners, while other professionals providing very similar services think of themselves as specialists in their particular disciplines. In this document, the term "early intervention professional" is used to mean any professional who provides early intervention services to children and families. This designation is not meant to exclude any professional or any discipline; in whatever way they identify themselves, all those serving infants and toddlers with special needs have an important contribution to make to the IFSP process.

Professionals must be willing to go beyond the narrow boundaries of their disciplines or agencies and to reach out to others who are also planning or providing services to these children and their families. Public Law 99-457 provided a timely reminder that the field of early intervention is multidisciplinary -- made up of professionals from education, health, mental health, and social services who are concerned with comprehensive developmental services to infants and young children with special needs and their families.

The IFSP component of the law challenges professionals and families to work together in new ways. At the state planning level, Part H grantees and other state agencies are searching for innovative approaches to interagency coordination. At the local level, families and service providers are developing community responses to the IFSP. All are continuing to search for best practices for Individualized Family Service Plans.

As this body of information grows, policy makers and practitioners are taking a new approach to working with infants and toddlers and their families. In like manner, families are creating new opportunities to develop partnerships with professionals. Past practices and approaches are being examined and refined in light of newly emerging family-centered philosophies, models, and program practices. These approaches can then be directed toward enabling and empowering families to enhance the development of their children with special needs and toward preventing families and children from becoming isolated from friends and community.

Evolution of the Monograph

To help state planners, families, and practitioners develop IFSP policies and procedures that are consistent with emerging best practices, the Office of Special Education and Rehabilitative Services (OSERS) of the U.S. Department of Education initiated several activities that resulted in the development of the first edition of this monograph.

Call to the Field for Exemplary Practices

As a first step, the Office of Special Education and Rehabilitative Services, working collaboratively with the Maternal and Child Health Bureau and the Administration on Developmental Disabilities, issued a call to the field in October 1987, to identify exemplary IFSP practices and formats. Notices were sent to state departments of health and special education; universities and University Affiliated Programs; Parent Training and Information Centers and other parent organizations; and early intervention programs and practitioners asking for submissions of materials related to best practices for the IFSP process, including philosophical statements, assessment tools, IFSP formats, and sample IFSPs.

The wide variety of responses to this call highlighted a need to gather and explore best practices for the IFSP. An Expert Team and Task Force was formed for this purpose.

The Expert Team and Task Force

The National Early Childhood Technical Assistance System (NEC*TAS) at the University of North Carolina at Chapel Hill appointed the Expert Team to develop a document to help state and local policy makers, personnel preparation programs, early intervention professionals, and families as they plan, implement, and evaluate IFSP procedures. The Expert Team was composed of both parents and professionals.

The Expert Team worked in conjunction with a Task Force composed of representatives from all of the federal departments and offices involved in services to young children with special needs and their families, state planners, university personnel preparation faculty, and parents and service providers from across the country. The Task Force members represented racial, ethnic, and geographic diversity. Among the disciplines and perspectives represented were advocacy, child development, law, medicine, nursing, occupational therapy, physical therapy, psychology, social work, special education, and speech and language pathology. A list of Expert Team and Task Force members is provided in the Foreword, along with more information about the process used to develop the first edition of this monograph.

This first edition of this document represented an emerging consensus about current best practices for providing family-centered, comprehensive early intervention services. Because states and programs differ in the ways they have served, or will serve, infants and toddlers with special needs and their families, the monograph did not attempt to provide a blueprint for implementation. Rather, it suggested a philosophy and conceptual framework for the IFSP and recommended practices and procedures consistent with state-of-the-art, family-centered early intervention.

More than 7,000 copies of *Guidelines and Recommended Practices for the Individualized Family Service Plan* were distributed to lead agencies, Part H planners, Interagency Coordinating Councils (ICC), personnel preparation programs, early intervention programs and providers, and parent and family organizations. The principles articulated in the monograph have been used in many states as a foundation for their IFSP work -- in Part H and ICC mission statements, in state and local IFSP task forces, in university training programs, in family advocacy efforts, and in local early intervention programs.

The Second Edition

Guidelines and Recommended Practices for the Individualized Family Service Plan was published before the Department of Education released the final regulations for Public Law 99-457 and before most states had begun significant work on IFSP policies and procedures. When it was time to reprint the book, NEC*TAS and ACCH decided to collaborate on a new edition that would include the final IFSP regulations and an update on IFSP best practices.

This new edition does not attempt to provide a comprehensive report on how states are implementing the IFSP component of Part H. Such information is available from NEC*TAS and from the Carolina Policy Studies Program, both at the Frank Porter Graham Child Development Center, University of North Carolina at Chapel Hill. It does, however, include new resources and new examples of creative IFSP approaches being developed in states and programs across the country.

Overview of the Monograph

Chapter Two, "Philosophy and Conceptual Framework," suggests principles and concepts that are critical to developing a family-centered philosophy and conceptual framework for the IFSP. Among the issues addressed are definitions of "family," the importance of culturally competent services, principles for enabling and supporting families, and a collaborative team approach to the IFSP. The necessary components of the IFSP, as outlined in Part H, are listed, and the regulations related to the IFSP are summarized.

Chapter Three, "The IFSP Sequence," describes a family-centered process for IFSP development. This process typically begins with the first contacts between a family and early intervention services and continues throughout assessment, outcome development, implementation, and evaluation. A diagram of an interactive, nonlinear process for the IFSP is provided. Because children and families enter early intervention for different reasons and through a variety of routes, four vignettes illustrating this diversity are provided. The experiences of the children and families highlighted in these vignettes are used as examples throughout the document to clarify the IFSP process.

Chapter Four, "Building Positive Relationships Between Professionals and Families," addresses the interactions between families and professionals that shape the character of early intervention. The composition of the IFSP team is outlined, and the family's role as final decision maker is discussed. The impact of the values and beliefs that both staff and families bring to the team process is acknowledged. Additionally, the importance of collaboration and negotiation is stressed.

Chapter Five, "Identifying Children's Strengths and Needs," discusses current best practices for identifying a child's strengths, needs, and resources as part of a family-centered IFSP process. Principles and guidelines for nonintrusive assessment approaches are presented and professional and family roles are discussed.

Because of the long history of programs and practitioners with child assessment and the wealth of material and training available in this area, this chapter does not attempt to break new ground in child assessment. Rather, it outlines principles and practices consistent with family-centered assessment approaches. A NEC*TAS-convened Expert Team on screening and assessment of infants and toddlers produced a document in this area, *Screening and Assessment: Guidelines for Identifying Young Disabled and Developmentally Vulnerable Children and Their Families* (Meisels & Provence, 1989).

Chapter Six, "Identifying Family Concerns, Priorities, and Resources," addresses family-centered approaches to helping families identify those family concerns, priorities, and resources that they determine are "related to enhancing the development" of their infant or toddler with special needs {1477(d)(2)}. The strictly voluntary and individualized aspects of this IFSP activity are stressed. Consistent with emerging best practice, the chapter emphasizes family self-identification of priorities and choices and of the resources available and necessary to bring about those choices.

Chapter Seven, "Outcomes, Strategies, Activities, and Services," provides guidelines for developing IFSP outcomes, selecting the strategies and activities that will be used to bring about those outcomes, and negotiating the early intervention services that support the outcomes. "Outcomes" is defined and distinguished from "goals and objectives." Family and staff responsibilities are discussed, and procedures that enable and support families are outlined.

Chapter Eight, "Implementing the Individualized Family Service Plan," outlines key concepts and procedures for implementing and evaluating the IFSP in local programs and communities. The case management, or service coordination, provision in the IFSP is discussed; recommended practices are suggested; and a process for protection of family rights is outlined. This monograph does not attempt to address fully all issues of importance to service coordination and IFSP implementation, because to do so was not the mission of this Expert Team and Task Force.

Chapter Nine, "Future Directions for the IFSP," updates and summarizes the implications of the Individualized Family Service Plan component for state planners and policy makers, for personnel preparation programs, for service providers, and for families. The continuing need for family/professional collaboration and interagency and interdisciplinary coordination and cooperation is stressed.

Key terms used in this document are defined in the **Glossary**. Also defined are any terms that might be considered professional jargon. It may be helpful for readers to peruse the Glossary before reading the body of the monograph.

The **Appendices** include additional materials to assist with the IFSP process. Sample IFSPs, updated to be consistent with the regulations, are provided for the four families described in the vignettes and followed throughout the document. Also provided are family-centered principles, guidelines, and checklists; sample forms and procedures; copies of instruments for identifying family concerns, priorities, and resources; and sample family satisfaction measures.

Use of the Monograph

This document contains suggested guidelines and recommendations for those who are responsible for implementing family-centered IFSP policies and procedures. As the work of many parents and professionals from diverse states, disciplines, and backgrounds, it represents a growing consensus on a family-centered process for the IFSP. This document also reflects the consensus of the Expert Team and Task Force members. Though individual members may differ in their beliefs, emphases, and priorities, the entire group supports the philosophy and principles included in the monograph.

Although such diversity ensures that a variety of concerns and viewpoints are represented in this book, no one document can provide all the answers. Each state is now developing IFSP policies and guidelines for its local programs. Local programs and families are using those state guidelines and regulations to develop policies and procedures for implementing the IFSP requirement in a way that supports, rather than supplants, the caregiving role of families.

In the almost two years since the first edition of this book was published, the family-centered principles advanced by the original Expert Team and Task Force have become the standard of practice in many states. Many of the finer points of family-centered practice that some found revolutionary when the first edition was published have since become commonly accepted IFSP practice.

The coming years will undoubtedly continue to yield much discussion and further field-testing of IFSP principles and best practices. Early intervention program staff can use this monograph and other materials to examine all aspects of their program practice and to refine their work with families in light of the continued evolution of best practices for the IFSP. At the policy level, families can use the document to collaborate on the development of responsive early intervention systems, programs, and services. At the service delivery level, families can use the document to ensure the development of Individualized Family Service Plans that match family concerns, priorities, resources, and choices.

Philosophy and Conceptual Framework

By Mary J. McGonigel

Introduction

The development of an IFSP process that supports, rather than supplants, the caregiving role of families is a complex task involving many people. Despite the variety of perspectives that are necessarily reflected in this process, it is critically important that all those involved share a family-centered philosophy and conceptual framework. The requirement in the law for an Individualized Family Service Plan for all children and families receiving early intervention services validates the principle that infants and toddlers with special needs must be served within the context of their families.

In recent years, a family-centered philosophy has steadily gained acceptance in early intervention. By the time Public Law 99-457 was passed, there was near unanimity among early intervention organizations and practitioners on the primary importance of the family, as evidenced in the testimony provided to Congress and in the Congressional Report (Gilkerson, Hilliard, Schrag, & Shonkoff, 1987).

State planners and policy makers, personnel preparation faculty, early intervention professionals, families, and others involved in implementing the IFSP provision are exploring the implications of adopting a family-centered approach in all areas of services to infants and toddlers with special needs and their families. This chapter examines the implications of a family-centered approach to the IFSP, suggests principles that can be used as a conceptual framework for developing IFSP policies and procedures, raises a critical question related to the IFSP, outlines the IFSP components required by the law, and summarizes the IFSP regulations.

Each suggested principle is followed by a short narrative. References from the literature are included that may be helpful to those engaged in developing IFSP policies and procedures for their states and programs.

Principles Underlying The IFSP Process

The individual needs and circumstances of each state and program influence the specific IFSP policies and procedures they choose to adopt. If family-centered early intervention is to become a reality, however, there are a few commonly shared principles that form a framework for IFSP policies and procedures that will enable and empower families as they invite early intervention programs into their lives.

"Enable" and "empower" are words that have gained increasing acceptance as terms embodying both the spirit and the heart of family-centered services (Dunst & Trivette, 1987; Shelton, Jeppson, & Johnson, 1987). Because these terms are used in a variety of ways in early intervention and in everyday speech, it may be helpful to define the way in which they are used in this document.

Enabling families means creating opportunities and means for families to apply their present abilities and competencies and to acquire new ones as necessary to meet their needs and the needs of their children (Dunst, Trivette, & Deal, 1988). *Empowerment* is both a process and an outcome that takes different forms in different families (Rappaport, 1984). Empowering families in early intervention does not mean giving or bestowing power on families -- the power is theirs by right. Rather, it means interacting with families in such a way that they maintain or acquire a sense of control over their family life and attribute positive changes that result from early intervention to their own strengths, abilities, and actions (Dunst, Trivette, et al., 1988).

A first step for states and programs developing an IFSP process may be an exploration and consensus-seeking discussion of the following principles. These principles are rooted in the belief that family-centered early intervention seeks to build on and promote the strengths and competencies present in all families.

- **Infants and toddlers are uniquely dependent on their families for their survival and nurturance. This dependence necessitates a family-centered approach to early intervention.**

From birth, an infant depends on adults to meet all of his needs, both physical and psychological. Getting these needs met requires the systematic development of interactive, loving relationships with adults. This unique, total dependence means that early intervention is an intimate service (Healy, et al., 1989) and that infants must be served within the context of their families.

A family-centered approach encourages researchers, practitioners, and families to recognize that an infant or toddler with special needs is part of her family system, which in turn is part of a larger network of informal and formal support systems. This systems approach to early intervention is rapidly becoming a foundation for best practice (Bailey, 1987; Dunst, 1985; Foster, Berger, & McLean, 1981). A family-centered systems approach to the IFSP acknowledges the importance of family direction in all aspects of service delivery -- that is, the family as the center of services and as the people who determine and direct how early intervention will be involved in their family life.

- **States and programs should define "family" in a way that reflects the diversity of family patterns and structures.**

As states and programs develop policies and procedures for implementing the IFSP provision in a family-centered way, a critical step is determining who will be considered "family" and, therefore, be eligible for early intervention services. The most inclusive definition of family moves beyond traditional and legal definitions to encompass primary nurturing caregivers and others who assume major, long-term roles in a child's daily life (Woodruff, McGonigel, Garland, et al., 1985). Examples of other persons who may play a long-term role in a child's life include sisters and brothers, cousins who live in the same house, or a trusted neighbor who becomes an "aunt."

Hartman (1981) suggested defining family as "two or more individuals who define themselves as a family and who, over time, assume those obligations to one another that are generally considered an essential component of family systems" (p. 8). This open-ended definition means that each family is able to define itself according to its own interpretation of who belongs to the family.

The value of inclusive definitions of "family" has been increasingly recognized in recent years. In the *Report of the House Memorial 5 Task Force on Young Children and Families* (1990) in New Mexico, family was described in the broadest possible terms:

> Families are big, small, extended, nuclear, multi-generational, with one parent, two parents, and grandparents. We live under one roof or many. A family can be as temporary as a few weeks, as permanent as forever. We become part of a family by birth, adoption, marriage, or from a desire for mutual support. . . . A family is a culture unto itself, with different values and unique ways of realizing its dreams; together, our families become the source of our rich cultural heritage and spiritual diversity. . . . Our families create neighborhoods, communities, states, and nations. (p. 1)

Weinstein (1979) described the success of an inclusive approach to family -- the use of an ecological model to provide services to inner-city families of color in Los Angeles:

> Our findings suggest that the nuclear family is not a sufficient model for the concept of family in all communities, and that we must respect the extended family by maintaining its integrity and utilizing its members whenever

necessary for the growth and development of . . . children. (p. 27)

Adopting such inclusive definitions makes it possible for a family to choose which of its members will be a part of the IFSP process and to use the strengths and resources that are already present in its support network. It is not intended to replace the primacy of the parent(s) or legal guardian(s) as the final decision maker in the IFSP process.

- **Each family has its own structure, roles, values, beliefs, and coping styles. Respect for and acceptance of this diversity is a cornerstone of family-centered early intervention.**

Respect for family diversity ensures that the IFSP process is supportive of each family's efforts to nurture and support its infant or toddler with special needs, while at the same time attending to the needs of the entire family. Respecting and accepting family diversity means acknowledging that there are strengths and resources present in all families. Therefore, early intervention professionals must learn to recognize and build on these positives as part of their work with families (Dunst, Trivette, et al., 1988; May, 1991; Shelton et al., 1987; Turnbull & Turnbull, 1986).

This approach holds equally true for all families, regardless of their ethnicity, cultural background, or socioeconomic circumstances. Richardson (1979) explored the implications of this principle in her description of an early intervention program in the Pediatrics Department of Drew Postgraduate Medical School in Los Angeles:

> We assume that any group of families or any individual family is as deeply caring and capable as any other group or individual family. We also assume that . . . all families want every possible chance for their children, and try to provide every opportunity and supportive strategy which they believe is necessary to their infant's development. (pp. 15-16)

- **Early intervention systems and strategies must honor the racial, ethnic, cultural, and socioeconomic diversity of families.**

American society is made up of people of many colors, cultures, ethnic origins, religions, and beliefs. Early intervention services generally, and the IFSP

Principles Underlying the IFSP Process

- Infants and toddlers are uniquely dependent on their families for their survival and nurturance. This dependence necessitates a family-centered approach to early intervention.
- States and programs should define "family" in a way that reflects the diversity of family patterns and structures.
- Each family has its own structure, roles, values, beliefs, and coping styles. Respect for and acceptance of this diversity is a cornerstone of family-centered early intervention.
- Early intervention systems and strategies must honor the racial, ethnic, cultural, and socioeconomic diversity of families.
- Respect for family autonomy, independence, and decision making means that families must be able to choose the level and nature of early intervention's involvement in their lives.
- Family/professional collaboration and partnerships are the keys to family-centered early intervention and to successful implementation of the IFSP process.
- An enabling approach to working with families requires that professionals reexamine their traditional roles and practices and develop new practices when necessary -- practices that promote mutual respect and partnerships.
- Early intervention services should be flexible, accessible, and responsive to family-identified needs.
- Early intervention services should be provided according to the normalization principle -- that is, families should have access to services provided in as normal a fashion and environment as possible and that promote the integration of the child and family within the community.
- No one agency or discipline can meet the diverse and complex needs of infants and toddlers with special needs and their families. Therefore, a team approach to planning and implementing the IFSP is necessary.

particularly, must reflect an awareness of and respect for these differences. When translated into action, this principle is known as cultural competence.

Cultural competence is a proactive concept that transcends traditional notions such as cultural sensitivity. Cross (1988) defined cultural competence as:

> a set of congruent behaviors, attitudes and policies that come together in a system, agency or professional and enable that system, agency or professional to work effectively in cross-cultural situations. . . . A culturally competent system of care acknowledges and incorporates -- at all levels -- the importance of culture, the assessment of cross cultural relations, vigilance toward the dynamics that result from cultural differences, the expansion of cultural knowledge and the adaptation of services to meet culturally unique needs. (p. 1)

In a culturally competent early intervention system, planners and program administrators develop early intervention options that match a family's language, culture, and spiritual beliefs. Among the most common provisions should be providing translators, hiring bilingual staff and staff from the cultures and communities being served, translating forms and other written materials, and providing staff with systematic, continuing inservice training on cultural perspectives in areas of particular importance in early intervention. Hanson and her colleagues (1990) identified six such topical areas for cross-cultural learning by staff: "views of children and childrearing, views of disability and its causation, views of change and intervention, views of medicine and healing, views of the family and family roles, and language and communication styles" (p. 114).

Families across all ethnic and racial groups, if they live in poverty, share many things in common. For example, by necessity, some low income families lead crisis-centered lives that are based on day-to-day survival rather than on long term planning -- very different from the middle class ideal. They may live in multi-generational households where age-defined roles may differ greatly from the middle class, and they may not share the same self-assurance that they can affect their world in positive ways (D. A. Jones, personal communication, February 1991). A middle class professional and a family living in poverty may bring these and many other differences in perspectives and experiences to their early intervention partnership. To truly honor the diversity of families, therefore, professionals need to be aware of how their own socioeconomic backgrounds affect their attitudes, beliefs, and behaviors (Wayman, Lynch, & Hanson, 1990).

- **Respect for family autonomy, independence, and decision making means that families must be able to choose the level and nature of early intervention's involvement in their lives.**

To support, rather than supplant, the caregiving roles of families, professionals should seek to promote a family's autonomy. Families must be able to choose how early intervention will be involved in their lives -- a choice based on their values, beliefs, resources, strengths, needs, and aspirations (McGonigel & Garland, 1988). Family autonomy and independence is promoted when professionals refrain from making decisions for families and from providing services that can be provided or arranged for by families (Dunst, 1987; Garland, Osborne, & Buck, 1988; Shelton et al., 1987). The IFSP should reflect families' choices for themselves and their children.

In recent years, many early intervention programs have begun to offer an array or menu of participation and service options from which families can select those that match their own values and priorities. Project Dakota in Minnesota was one such program:

> Project Dakota proposed a service menu format to stimulate creativity and flexibility in designing the who, how, what, and where of interventions in home, community, and center. The location, frequency, and nature of early intervention services may need to be as diverse as the children and families themselves. (L. Kjerland, personal communication, November 1988)

The Project Dakota Service Menu encouraged integrated services with non-delayed peers and included home-, center-, and community-based services. Community-based locations included family child care, nursery school, neighborhood play groups with staff help, church groups, recreation programs, and group lessons such as swimming and tumbling.

Such an IFSP approach is clearly consistent with respect for family autonomy and independence and with acknowledged best practice in early intervention. Families, however, must be able to choose for themselves services that may not be included in such an array or menu. Families and professionals must have opportunities to create unique and individually meaningful strategies and programs.

- **Family/professional collaboration and partnerships are the keys to family-centered early intervention and to successful implementation of the IFSP process.**

Collaboration and partnerships are essential at all levels of developing and evaluating early intervention services -- from the policy, planning, and personnel preparation levels to the service delivery level. Learning to collaborate with families may require new attitudes and new skills on the part of professionals -- attitudes and skills that allow professionals to recognize and build on family competence and resourcefulness (Bailey, 1987; Dunst, Trivette, et al., 1988; Shelton et al., 1987). Families also may need to learn new skills as they assume more collaborative roles in their interactions with professionals.

A collaborative approach does not mean, however, that families and professionals have equal authority in IFSP decision making. Respect for family autonomy and for the primacy of family beliefs, values, and choices dictates that, except in those rare instances that involve child abuse or neglect as defined by federal and state statutes, families have the final decision in all matters regarding their children. In a truly collaborative approach to the IFSP, the right of families to make decisions for their children and themselves exists in harmony with the responsibility of professionals to share their knowledge, expertise, and concerns with families who seek early intervention services.

- **An enabling approach to working with families requires that professionals reexamine their traditional roles and practices and develop new practices when necessary -- practices that promote mutual respect and partnerships.**

The move toward family-centered early intervention represents a profound shift of perspective for many professionals whose training and practice has equipped them to work primarily with children and whose role with families has been primarily an instructive one. Dunst, Trivette, et al. (1988) identified eight non-mututally exclusive roles that may be helpful to practitioners as they reexamine their professional roles: empathetic listener, teacher/therapist, consultant, resource, enabler, mobilizer, mediator, and advocate.

An enabling approach should inform every aspect of the IFSP process. Dunst, Trivette, et. al. (1988) developed twelve guidelines for enabling and empowering families in early intervention. The guidelines translate the principles developed through research at the Family, Infant and Preschool Program into family-centered practices. These guidelines are provided for reference in Appendix B. Also included in Appendix B are the key elements of family-centered care as articulated by the National Center for Family-Centered Care at the Association for the Care of Children's Health and a description of the major categories of family support as identified by Dunst and colleagues at the Center for Family Studies.

- **Early intervention services should be flexible, accessible, and responsive to family-identified needs.**

Family-centered early intervention requires that services be developed with the individuality of families in mind. Services should be "tailor made" to suit the specific strengths, needs, resources, and choices of each child and family (Kjerland, 1987). Rather than asking families to adjust to program needs and policies, early intervention programs should adapt their policies and services to the needs of the families they are designed to serve. The IFSP should reflect the services families say they need and want rather than the services the program wants to offer.

Dokecki and Heflinger (1989) called such an approach to meeting child and family needs under Public Law 99-457 "mapping backward from the street level" (p. 59). Rather than planning services from the top down, with agency structures and organization determining available services, a backward mapping approach dictates that services

New roles for professionals in early intervention can include: empathetic listener, teacher/therapist, consultant, resource, enabler, mobilizer, mediator, and advocate (Dunst, Trivette, & Deal, 1988).

be planned from the consumer level up. Consumer needs are the driving force, and agency policies and structures that are necessary to meet such needs are put into place. Such a consumer-driven perspective is essential to family-centered services.

- **Early intervention services should be provided according to the normalization principle -- that is, families should have access to services that are provided in as normal a fashion and environment as possible and that promote the integration of the child and family within the community.**

There is much debate over the concept of "least restrictive environment" for infants and toddlers. Although Part H does not deal with this concept in depth, the normalization principle is clearly consistent with the intent of the legislation.

Many parents of young children with special needs say that they feel isolated from normal community life when the only activities in which their children participate are those specifically for children with special needs. IFSP outcomes and strategies that include typical community activities help promote interdependence and a sense of belonging for these children and their families.

Interdependence is strengthened when IFSPs emphasize natural family supports within the community such as neighbors, churches, and community clubs. Interdependence, reciprocal obligations, and supportive exchanges with their own communities are the best contexts for strengthening families and promoting human development (Dunst, Trivette, Gordon, et al., 1989; Hobbs, Dokecki, Hoover-Dempsey, et al., 1984).

- **No one agency or discipline can meet the diverse and complex needs of infants and toddlers with special needs and their families. Therefore, a team approach to planning and implementing the IFSP is necessary.**

This principle, in fact, is part of the legislation that establishes the IFSP requirement. Although the law requires that the family and professionals from multiple disciplines be involved in the IFSP process, it does not provide guidance concerning the roles and relationships among the team* members who will implement the IFSP process.

In recent years, the early intervention literature has offered many discussions of various models for team interaction (Bailey, 1984; Woodruff & McGonigel, 1988). Now that Part H requires a team approach, programs have an excellent opportunity to examine their team functioning in light of a family-centered approach. Creative redesign of traditional team models is strengthening family role choices and options. For example, family empowerment on early intervention teams is a major emphasis of Project Trans/Team Outreach, a training and technical assistance project funded by the Early Education Program for Children with Disabilities (EEPCD), at Child Development Resources in Lightfoot, Virginia.

In addition to teams operating within an early intervention program, multiagency teams are a critical aspect of a comprehensive, coordinated system of early intervention. The absence of such coordination among local early intervention, education, health, mental health, and social service agencies will limit the possibilities of the IFSP process and will make comprehensive support to families and their infants and toddlers with special needs an unfulfilled promise.

Project WIN Outreach, an EEPCD funded training and technical assistance project in greater Boston, is demonstrating the effectiveness of transagency models in coordinating comprehensive early intervention and family support services to children with HIV infection and their families (Woodruff, Hanson, McGonigel, & Sterzin, 1990). Such a transagency approach has potential in many other aspects of family-centered early intervention and IFSP implementation.

***Note:** The word "team" when used in this document *always* refers to the family and professionals. It is *never* used to mean professional members of the team only.

A Critical Question

Part H and its regulations leave many critical issues up to individual states to decide. One of the most important decisions still to be made by many states and programs is their response to the following question: "Do early intervention programs have a responsibility to help families meet their needs beyond those that have traditionally been considered part of early intervention such as food, clothing, housing, or employment?"

In other words, how will state planners and local early intervention programs interpret the Part H statement that the IFSP will address strengths and needs "relating to enhancing the development of the family's infant or toddler with disabilities" {1477(d)(2)}? The answer to this question will help determine both the boundaries of the IFSP and the success of Part H in meeting the "urgent and substantial need" to "enhance the capacity of families to meet the special needs of their infants and toddlers with disabilities" {1471(a)}.

A family-centered response to this question may require that early intervention itself be defined in a new way, as:

> the provision of support (i.e., resources provided by others) by members of a family's informal and formal social network that either directly or indirectly influences child, parent, and family functioning. (Dunst, Trivette, et al., 1988, p. 5)

Family-centered early intervention addresses all the pressing needs that families identify (Bailey, 1988; Dunst, Trivette, et al., 1988; Garland, Woodruff, & Buck, 1988) -- either directly or through linkages and referral services, with the service coordinator helping families gain access to needed services.

Content of the IFSP and Final Regulations

Part H of Public Law 101-476 (formerly 99-457), Section 1477, specifies the content of the IFSP and certain requirements for participation and implementation. The final regulations -- Federal Register, Department of Education, 34 CFR, Part 303 -- elaborate on the IFSP requirements as specified in the statute itself.

The regulations include requirements for every aspect of the IFSP component of the statewide early intervention program. Among these are evaluation and assessment; lead agency responsibilities; definition of early intervention services; general roles of service providers; time frames for IFSP development, implementation, and review; provisions for procedural safeguards; participants in and conduct of the IFSP meeting; case management;* and early provision of services. It is beyond the scope of this document to discuss the many regulations governing the IFSP. Readers are referred directly to the regulations published in the *Federal Register* for June 22, 1989, and to *Early Intervention Regulation: Annotation and Analysis of Part H* (Brown, 1990), a sourcebook on the law and regulations.

The contents of the IFSP, as outlined in the statute, Section 1477(d), and some clarifying information from the regulations are provided in the following paragraphs. Additional information from the regulations is provided in the appropriate chapters throughout this document.

The IFSP must be a written plan developed by a multidisciplinary team, including the parent(s) or guardian(s) that contains the following:

- a statement of the infant's or toddler's present levels of physical development, cognitive development, language and speech development, psycho-social development, and self-help skills, based on acceptable objective criteria;

  (Regulations specify vision, hearing, and health status as aspects of physical development that must be included in the statement of the child's present level of development. {303.344(a)})

***Note:** Part H and the regulations, in their current form, use the term "case management," so this discussion of the law and regulations uses "case management" also. Elsewhere in the book, the more family-centered term "service coordination" is used.

- a statement of the family's strengths and needs relating to enhancing the development of the family's infant or toddler with a disability;

  (Regulations clarify that this activity should be based on information provided by the family and that identification of family strengths and needs is voluntary on the part of the family. {303.322(d)})

- a statement of the major outcomes expected to be achieved for the child and family; the criteria, procedures, and timelines used to determine the degree to which progress toward achieving the outcomes is being made, and whether revisions of the outcomes or services are necessary;

- a statement of specific early intervention services necessary to meet the unique needs of the infant or toddler and family, including the frequency, intensity, and method of delivering services;

  (Regulations specify that "payment arrangements, if any" must be included in the IFSP. {303.344 (d)} Regulations also require a statement of the location where a service is provided, for example, at home, at a center, in a hospital, or in other settings as appropriate.

  These same regulations further clarify that, to the extent possible, "other services" must be included in the IFSP, as well as, if necessary, the steps that will be taken to secure those services from public or private sources. Among these services are non-routine medical and other services that a child needs, but that are not required by Part H. Routine medical services such as "well-baby care" and immunizations should be included when a child needs such services and they are not provided or are not otherwise available. {303.344(e)})

- the projected dates for initiation of services and the anticipated duration of the services;

- the name of the case manager (from the profession most immediately relevant to the child's or family's needs) who will be responsible for implementing the plan and coordinating with other agencies and persons; and

  (Regulations clarify that case management can be considered a "profession." {303.344(g)})

- the steps to be taken supporting the child's transition to Part B preschool services, if appropriate.

  (Regulations clarify that the child's transition to other available services should be addressed, and require that transition support include discussion with and training of parents about transition issues, including future placements, and preparation of the child for changes in service delivery, including steps to help the child adjust to and function in a new setting. {303.344(h)})

Some of the above provisions are very similar to those traditionally addressed in early intervention service plans. Other provisions, particularly those related to identifying family strengths and needs and developing outcomes that match these strengths and needs, are new requirements for most programs.

Many state planners, families, and practitioners are still uncertain about exactly what these new requirements mean at the level of IFSP implementation. What is the best way to identify family strengths and needs? How will programs and agencies choose the family support services they offer? What should the IFSP team do when a family identifies needs and asks for help that a program is not able to provide or help the family arrange for? What happens when staff and families disagree on priorities for services?

This document suggests principles and guidelines for answering these and other questions in ways that are consistent with the family-centered early intervention principles described in this chapter.

The IFSP Sequence

By Mary J. McGonigel, Roxane K. Kaufmann, and Joicey L. Hurth

The process for developing the IFSP consists of the gathering, sharing, and exchange of information between families and staff to enable families to make informed choices about the early intervention services they want for their children and themselves.

Introduction

This chapter describes a family-centered process for developing and implementing the Individualized Family Service Plan provision of Part H and describes the four families whose experiences are used throughout the document to illustrate key concepts.

The IFSP process is more important than the plan itself. Family-centered early intervention is built on collaboration and partnerships between families and professionals. Without these partnerships the written plan becomes almost meaningless.

The IFSP process cannot be conceptualized as a simple, step-by-step progression. The preferences, concerns, desires, and choices of an individual family determine the nature and timing of the IFSP process. Figure 1 on the following page illustrates a dynamic process for developing and implementing Individualized Family Service Plans. Rather than the linear progression from component to component that has been typical in early intervention and true also of the Individualized Educational Program (IEP) process, each family moves through this dynamic IFSP process as befits its circumstances.

The IFSP process can begin at any point at which a child and family come into contact with professionals who are serving infants and young children. For example:

> Jesse Ortega became concerned about his daughter, Anna Maria. Although Anna was his first child and he wasn't sure what to expect, he was worried because she was five months old and still didn't seem to look at him when he talked to her. In fact, Anna never seemed to look at anything at all.
>
> Mr. Ortega called Anna Maria's pediatrician, Dr. Paloma Garcia, who told him to bring Anna in the next day. Dr. Garcia was concerned about Anna's vision and referred Anna and Mr. Ortega to Dr. Richard Darling, a pediatric ophthalmologist.
>
> After completing several tests, Dr. Darling diagnosed Anna as having no functional vision as a result of her undeveloped optic disc. He talked to Mr. Ortega for a long time about some of the implications of Anna's diagnosis and answered his many questions. At the end of the visit, Dr. Darling called the local early intervention program, with whom he frequently consulted, to introduce them to Mr. Ortega and to refer Anna Maria for services.

When Mr. Ortega called Anna's pediatrician, he had no idea that as a result of his call he and Anna would enter an early intervention program. Yet, the respect, information, and support he received from Dr. Garcia and Dr. Darling set the stage for positive future relationships with the many professionals that he and Anna would encounter in early intervention and in later school years. In a very real sense, the IFSP process for Anna and Mr. Ortega can be said

Figure 1
The IFSP Sequence

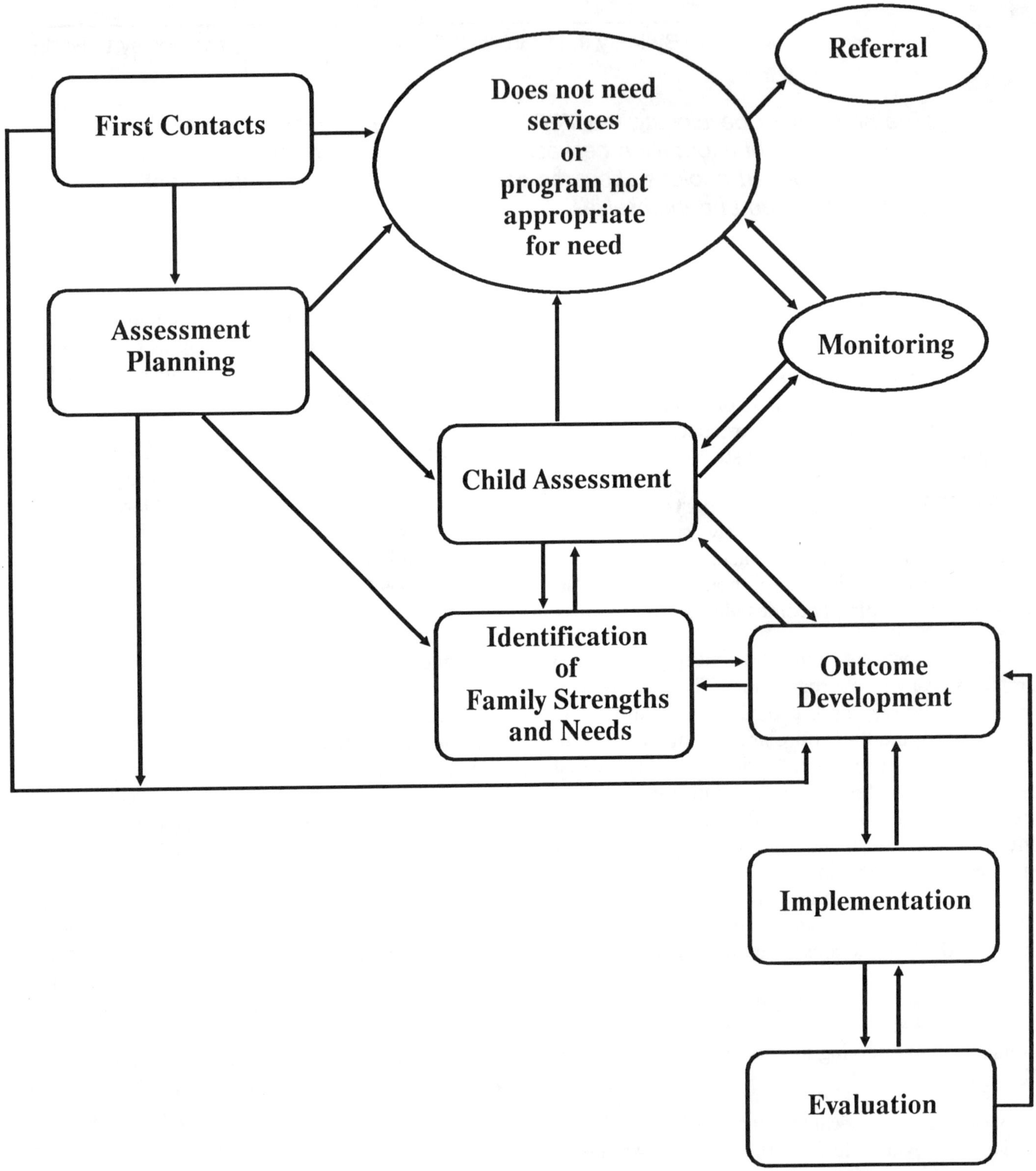

to have begun in the pediatrician's office. All those working with infants and toddlers and their families have the potential to affect the IFSP process for good or ill.

Overview of the Process

Regardless of the kind of agency or organization, the program model, or the eligibility criteria, several key activities occur as part of the IFSP process:

- first contacts between a family and early intervention services;
- assessment planning;
- child assessment;
- identification of family concerns, priorities, and resources;
- development of outcomes to meet child and family needs;
- IFSP implementation; and
- formal and informal evaluation of the IFSP and the IFSP process.

Although the components of the IFSP process are generally sequential, they are also interactive -- the information exchanged and the activities conducted in one aspect of the process affect the activities in all the other components in a nonlinear, back-and-forth fashion.

Each activity is described in the sections that follow. Those parts of the process that are described in subsequent chapters of this monograph are only touched on here. Other aspects are more fully discussed.

First Contacts

Referrals to early intervention services come from a number of sources, including hospital neonatal intensive care units (NICUs), local physicians or other health care providers, community-wide screening programs or well-baby clinics, social service or child protection programs, or other early intervention programs. Families also frequently refer themselves.

Once a child or family has been referred to an early intervention program, the first contacts between a family and the program take place. This process differs from program to program, but the traditional aim of these first contacts has been to gather preliminary information about the child and family in order to make an initial eligibility determination. A family-centered approach, however, emphasizes a much different aspect of first contacts.

If family preferences and priorities are to shape the IFSP process, then these preferences and priorities must be identified as early as possible. First contacts are discussed here at great length because of their importance to the entire family-centered process for developing the IFSP.

Identifying a Family's Agenda

Identifying families' agendas for themselves and their children begins during these first contacts between a family and program, but it is an activity that continues throughout assessment, outcome development and implementation, and evaluation. *A family's agenda -- its priorities for how early intervention will be involved in family life -- shapes the entire family-centered IFSP process.* This agenda tailors the process to an individual family's priorities, service history, and point of entry into early intervention.

The degree to which a family is able to identify and articulate its agenda varies from family to family and may depend on a number of circumstances, such as previous experiences with services or how recently a diagnosis was made. Some families will come to an early intervention program as part of a continuum of services that began in the NICU shortly after birth. The information and records available from the hospital can often substitute for the usual information gathered during first contacts and assessment planning, but this information should be reviewed with the family to ensure that it is accurate and unbiased.

Families entering early intervention from other services often have a great deal of information about their children's strengths and needs and may know exactly what they would like from an early intervention program. Many are able, even at a first visit, to articulate their agendas for their children and themselves and to define the outcomes they want to form the base of their IFSPs. The following example describes one such family:

> Manuel DeLeon was born very early, with respiratory and gastrointestinal problems. Surgery corrected part of his gastrointestinal problems, but he still needs to be fed through a nasogastric (NG) tube. The DeLeons were able to visit Manuel every day when he was in the NICU. Their hospital team showed them how to cuddle Manuel and read his behavioral cues. After three months in the NICU, Manuel no longer needed supplemental oxygen, and plans were made for his discharge.
>
> Before Manuel went home, the DeLeons learned all about NG feeding and caring for the equipment that Manuel would need at home. The physicians, nursing staff, and the other members of their medical team taught them everything they wanted to know about how to care for Manuel.
>
> A child development specialist who consults in the NICU assessed Manuel's development. In discussing her findings with Mr. & Mrs. DeLeon, she suggested that Manuel would benefit from having his development monitored regularly by an early intervention program.
>
> The DeLeons invited someone from the early intervention program in their community to come to the hospital to meet the family and to talk about the services they might want from the program. In discussion with the early intervention program staff member, the DeLeons decided that they would like to have Manuel monitored by the program. Manuel's assessment in the NICU was determined to be adequate for purposes of program entry and the IFSP process. Because they were already participating in a parent support group at the hospital, the DeLeons decided that, for now, they wanted only monitoring services from the early intervention program.

The DeLeon family needed little or no help identifying their initial priorities for themselves and their baby. The priorities they identified during their first contacts with the program became their IFSP outcomes, as the DeLeons moved directly from first contacts to outcome development.

Other families encounter services for the first time following their referral to a community-based early intervention program. Many times these parents have only just learned that their child may have a developmental problem. They may have no information about early intervention, and, thus, they may not have considered what services they would like for their child and themselves. The exchange of information between the family and program may focus on answering family questions and discussing basic concerns. The Christophers are one such family:

> Robin and Mae Christopher were referred to a local early intervention program by their pediatrician when their daughter, Winnie, was born with Down syndrome. Winnie was the Christophers' first child, and they were uncertain about their child care skills in general, as well as concerned about Winnie's special needs related to her Down syndrome.
>
> When someone from the early intervention program first visited them at home, Mr. & Mrs. Christopher told the home visitor that they were shocked when Winnie was born with a problem and that they did not know what they were supposed to do. They had many questions about Winnie's potential for development. Would she be able to graduate from high school and work at a job she enjoyed? Would she be able to get married and have children of her own?
>
> The Christophers said that they wanted to give Winnie whatever she needed. They wanted to invite the early intervention program into their family life, but they were not sure what that meant right now. The home

visitor talked with the Christophers about planning an assessment to talk about Winnie and her development and about ways the program could be helpful to the whole family. She answered their questions about high school graduation, jobs, marriage, and children, and she suggested some adults in their community with Down syndrome who the Christophers might want to meet.

The Christophers had a broad sense of what they wanted for their baby and themselves in the future, but they needed help articulating their agenda and considering their immediate service priorities. The outcomes this family ultimately chose for its IFSP were the result of a great deal of consultation between the Christophers and the other members of their early intervention team as they went through the process of assessing Winnie and identifying family strengths and needs.

The IFSP process can strengthen family members' abilities to initiate life planning for their child with special needs. As a family begins to identify its agenda, early intervention professionals can help family members look to the future and think about their long range goals, both for their infant or toddler with special needs and for the entire family. Thinking about the future also can help a family plan for the immediate present, since family goals for a child's future can help determine the services family members would like from an early intervention program.

In their IFSP guidebook for families, *Into Our Lives*, developed at the Family Child Learning Center in Tallmadge, Ohio, Hunt and her coauthors advised other families on identifying their priorities as part of the IFSP process:

> As you participate in the planning process, you should be identifying your priorities -- those things that are important to you and your family. These priorities may include goals and dreams you have for your child and yourselves. (p. 26)

Table 1 lists some typical family priorities Hunt and her colleagues provided to help other families think about their own priorities for their children and themselves.

Table 1
Typical Family Priorities

For our child we want

- independence
- personal happiness
- feelings of accomplishment
- respect
- ability to walk
- ability to communicate
- good friends
- understanding that he/she is loved
- employment
- skills to feed him/herself
- skills to dress him/herself
- comfortable enough to sleep through the night
- skills to drive car
- the experience of having a loving relationship with a member of the opposite sex
- to know and love God

For our family we want

- social outings (especially restaurants)
- sleep-filled nights
- enjoyments of an evening out (as a couple)
- normal sibling relationships
- relatives and friends to understand the nature of our child's disabilities
- help with planning some adaptations to our home

Source: Hunt, M., Cornelius, P., Leventhal, P., et al. (1990). *Into our lives*. Akron, OH: Children's Hospital Medical Center.

Family Choices for Involvement and Information Sharing

A family's preference for how an early intervention program will become involved in its life will affect all other aspects of the IFSP process. Since there are many cultural styles, values, and family structures in American society, it is necessary to ask who are the important players in a family's life. These important persons may vary widely, as demonstrated by the experiences of one early intervention practitioner:

> A service coordinator invited Mrs. Lloyd to bring her family to a meeting to talk about planning an assessment. When Mrs. Lloyd arrived for the meeting, the people she brought along included her baby, her two other children, her boyfriend, her mother, her best friend, and her sister.
>
> When the same service coordinator invited Betty Chee, another mother, to bring her family to a meeting, she brought her husband Joe, her toddler, her eldest daughter, and a tribal elder -- an entirely different array of people.

An inclusive definition of "family" allows each family to define itself, and many families choose to have friends and extended family members be involved in the IFSP process. Yet, individual family members can disagree with each other about major decisions. In the final analysis, it is the parent(s) or legal guardian(s) who have the authority to make decisions for the child and family. The experience of the Leary family illustrates this point:

> Patrick and Tancy Leary are the young parents of Maggie, a medically fragile infant who has many severe special needs as the result of being born at 24 weeks gestation. The Learys are committed to getting every treatment for Maggie that is recommended by their neonatalogist. They visit her every day, holding her whenever they can. Patrick's mother also comes to visit Maggie, and the Learys have asked the NICU staff to consider her another resource for helping Maggie.
>
> Patrick's mother is concerned about Maggie's potential to live a normal life and about the financial and emotional costs to her son and daughter-in-law of having a child with so many problems. She feels they are making a mistake to seek every possible treatment for Maggie whenever she needs resuscitation. Patrick and Tancy feel that Maggie's grandmother is an important part of Maggie's life, but they strongly disagree with her wish that Maggie not be aggressively treated.
>
> Recently, the Learys have been meeting with a child development specialist who comes to the NICU to show them things they can do to help their daughter. Together, the Learys, the neonatalogist and NICU nurses, and the child development specialist developed an IFSP for Maggie that focuses on getting her stabilized after each setback and promoting her development when she is stable. As part of the Learys' team, Maggie's grandmother participates in carrying out the IFSP outcomes, but the other members of the team look to Patrick and Tancy, rather than to her, for all decisions.

Once family members have decided who wants to be involved, those members can discuss their preferred IFSP team roles. Both the composition of the team and the roles assumed by various family members may change over time as child and family priorities, concerns, and preferences change.

It is also up to a family to determine the pace and extent of how it will share its life with an early intervention program. Some families may be put off, intimidated, or embarrassed by being asked for financial information, a pregnancy history, or similar personal information during their first contacts with a program.

One mother related her experience when her son was referred to an early intervention program two years ago:

> I called the program and told the person who answered the phone about my son, Ricky. She was so helpful -- she told me a little

about the program and said she would have the home visitor call me right back. When the home visitor called a little later, she was also very friendly and supportive. After hearing about Ricky, she told me he would automatically qualify for the program because of his special needs. She offered to come out to the apartment to tell me some more about the program and to get some information from me if I was interested in the program.

Everything was going just fine during the visit, and I decided that I definitely wanted Ricky and me to be part of the program. Then the home visitor started asking me questions that she said were required as part of something called "intake." She asked me lots of general questions that I didn't mind answering, but she also asked me if I had ever had an abortion, if I took any illegal drugs during my pregnancy, if my boyfriend who lives with me was Ricky's father, and how much money he made. I was so embarrassed! I guess I understood that her agency required her to ask those questions, but we don't talk about those kinds of things in my family -- at least not with strangers. I was sorry I ever called the program in the first place!

All questions that families are routinely asked should be carefully reviewed, and an explicit rationale should be stated for every question. The rationale should state why it is the business of a professional or an early intervention program to know the answer to the question. Questions that do not have a sufficient rationale should never be asked. Any question that a family finds threatening or intrusive should be addressed (if at all) only after the family and staff have established a relationship and family members have indicated that they are comfortable with the question.

Sharing Information with Families

Providing the family with initial information about early intervention services is an activity that requires thoughtful preparation by program staff, who must be careful not to limit a family by the way in which they describe services. At this early stage of its contact with a program, a family may be overly influenced to think of its needs, priorities, and preferences only in terms of existing services.

> Communication can be improved if professionals explained more fully why they are asking certain questions and if they are sensitive to parents' reactions. Parents can enhance the communication process by helping professionals to understand how best to ask questions -- what is supportive and helpful, and what is intrusive.
>
> *Source:* Shelton, T., Jeppson, E., & Johnson, B. H. (1987). *Family-centered care for children with special health care needs* (p. 17). Washington, DC: Association for the Care of Children's Health.

Most families are not aware of the number and variety of services that might be available to them. Professionals can provide information about how services from multiple agencies can be chosen, obtained, and coordinated as part of the IFSP process. The following example refers to the IFSP vignette that is provided on pages 25-26.

Vignette #1 -- When Mrs. Crowder, her sister, her social worker from the hospital, and her teenage daughter, Julie, first met with the staff of the early intervention program, they talked about Mrs. Crowder's hopes and concerns for Mary, her daughter with AIDS, and for her whole family. As they talked, it became clear that many different agencies, professionals, and extended family members would need to become involved in the IFSP process if Mary's needs were to be met. The community mental health agency, the public health department, and the hospital were all necessary partners with the early intervention program and the family, and staff from these agencies eventually became a part of the IFSP implementation team. If, however, the early intervention program staff had taken a narrow view of the IFSP process, Mrs. Crowder may never have known about the many agencies and individuals that were available to her for support and assistance and the many options that she could choose from as she and the other team members began to consider the content of the IFSP.

Next Steps

In some programs, the first contacts between a family and the program take place over a period of weeks. In such programs, the staff and family spend time getting to know one another and identifying family priorities and concerns. In other programs, agency constraints, personnel shortages, long distances in rural areas, and similar circumstances may limit first contacts to an initial home visit or two, during which some decisions about next steps must be made.

Several decisions can be made during these first contacts. The following are the major categories of decisions typically made at this stage in the process:

- Based on family-identified needs or concerns, developmental screening instruments, clinical judgments, family reports, or previous assessments, the family and the staff can begin the next phase of the process, assessment planning.
- Based on the same kind of information, the staff and family can determine, without further assessment, that the child and family do not need early intervention services. In such instances, family members should be referred or linked to other resources that can help them with whatever concerns prompted the initial referral.
- A child and family can be found not to need services at the time of initial contacts, but concerns about future development may indicate a need for periodic rescreening or developmental checks, in case the child's development or his family's circumstances change.
- A child can be found to need further assessment or to need early intervention services, but her parents may decide that they do not want her to participate. In such cases the professionals should determine if the parents have been provided the information and support they need to make an informed choice and to understand the implications of their decision. The parents should be asked if they are willing to be contacted by the program again in the future, in case their decision changes.

Table 2
Early Provision of Services

- "With the parent's consent, early intervention services may commence prior to the completion" of the evaluation of the child {Section 1477(c)}. This provision should be used sparingly and appropriately.
- A preliminary IFSP should be developed, using the same family-centered process discussed in this document.
- Certain services may be prescribed before the assessment is completed (for example, physical therapy for a child with cerebral palsy).
- The child *still* must receive a multidisciplinary evaluation.
- Case management services can be provided and are important in ensuring that information is shared and family choices are honored.
- States must design a flexible system that balances the need for early services against waiting for an entire multidisciplinary evaluation.

Assessment Planning

The purpose of this component of the process is to allow family and staff -- the IFSP team -- to plan an assessment that will address family priorities and concerns. To plan such an assessment, the staff must gather enough information about the child to ensure that appropriate child assessment measures and procedures will be used.

Assessment planning is a continuation of the same kind of information gathering and exchange that takes place during first contacts, but the information is more directly focused on the upcoming child assessment. Any medical records or assessment data from other services that the family is willing to share can be used to help plan the assessment. Assessment planning is discussed at greater length in Chapter Five, "Identifying Children's Strengths and Needs."

Child Assessment

Child assessment is the part of the IFSP process that is likely most familiar to professionals. Although assessment processes vary from program to program according to the service model, and from child to child depending on age, developmental level, and other child characteristics, a family-centered assessment approach is one in which the information needs, agenda, and preferences of an individual family shape the choice of participants, measures, and procedures.

Assessment serves different purposes at different times during the IFSP process. The first assessment of a child may focus on diagnosis and evaluation, as well as on gathering information that will be used by family and staff to develop the IFSP. Particularly useful at this stage is the determination of specific health and medical conditions that can contribute to the child's developmental problems. Periodic reassessments of the child as the IFSP is implemented help evaluate the effectiveness of the IFSP in meeting the child's needs and also demonstrate child progress over time. Chapter Five discusses assessment for the IFSP in greater depth.

Identifying Family Concerns, Priorities, and Resources

If child assessment is quite familiar to early intervention professionals, the identification of family concerns, priorities, and resources is much less so. As programs develop their procedures for this aspect of the IFSP process, it is important to note that this component is *not* an assessment of the family itself. Rather, it is a process to help a family identify its "strengths and needs relating to enhancing the development of the family's infant or toddler with a disability" {1477(d)(2)}.

This Part H provision was intended to allow early intervention programs to serve children within the context of their families. Therefore, families must have continuing opportunities to explore and express their concerns and to identify both the resources they bring and the resources they need to meet these concerns. It was not intended to give professionals permission to intrude uninvited into family life.

Out of this same concern over possible intrusiveness, some professionals and families have been concerned over the timing of this aspect of the IFSP process. Bailey (in press) described this concern as based on the assumption that:

> [identifying family concerns, resources, and priorities] is a formal process that is an "add-on" to child assessment and will likely result in the divulgence of sensitive information that would not ordinarily be shared early in the acquaintance process. In reality, becoming acquainted and developing a trusting relationship cannot occur in the absence of information gathering. The key is whether the approach taken is overstructured and evaluative as compared to natural and supportive.

Recommended practices for this component of the IFSP process are provided in Chapter Six.

Outcomes, Strategies, Activities, and Services

In every step of the IFSP process, families and professionals share information and discuss options for services. It is at this step of the process that the IFSP team brings it all together by reviewing what they have learned, making choices among competing priorities, developing outcomes, and negotiating the strategies, activities, and services that will result in achievement of the outcomes.

The infant and toddler component of Public Law 99-457 did not mention goals or objectives. Rather,

Part H calls for "outcomes expected to be achieved for the infant or toddler and the family" {1477 (d)(3)}. The addition of the family as the legitimate center of early intervention services requires a new, more collaborative way of approaching service plans. To emphasize the difference between the IEP and the IFSP, the Expert Team and Task Force chose to use "outcome," the language of Part H in this document. A family-centered approach to the IFSP dictates that these outcomes be based on a family's identified agenda and on a synthesis of all the information gathered and shared by the family and staff during first contacts, assessment planning, child assessment, and identification of family concerns, priorities, and resources.

Chapter Seven provides more detail on this aspect of the IFSP process, suggesting practices for developing functional outcomes and the activities or strategies that support their achievement.

Implementation

Implementation of the IFSP is the next step in the process. As the family and staff carry out the activities and strategies that they developed to meet IFSP outcomes, they bring the IFSP to life. Case management, or service coordination, is the process that ensures coordinated IFSP implementation. Implementation should occur in ways that support and strengthen family functioning. Chapter Eight provides principles and guidelines for IFSP implementation.

Evaluation

As the IFSP is implemented, the family and service coordinator evaluate the appropriateness of the outcomes and the effectiveness of the plan in meeting child and family needs. In addition to evaluating their own IFSPs, families should have opportunities to evaluate the IFSP process and the early intervention program.

Families and staff use the information gathered from evaluation activities and periodic reassessments to refine and revise IFSP outcomes and the accompanying strategies and activities.

Family Vignettes

The following vignettes and the corresponding IFSPs that appear in Appendix A were developed to illustrate the concepts and practices recommended in this document. Two vignette families represent a composite of several families. In the other two vignettes, the people and circumstances are real, but information that made them personally identifiable has been changed. The Crowder family vignette was developed by Geneva Woodruff and Chris Hanson at Project WIN in Roxbury, Massachusetts and Elizabeth Jeppson at ACCH. The Griffin family vignette was developed by Nancy DiVenere at Parent-to-Parent of Vermont, in Winooski, Vermont. The Lain family vignette was developed by Corinne Garland, Deana Buck, and Adrienne Frank at Project Trans/Team, Child Development Resources, in Lightfoot, Virginia. The Mack family vignette was developed by Mary Anne Sampon, Jeanette Myers, and Andrea Alder at Project LIFT of the Portage Projects, in Portage, Wisconsin, and George Jesien, now at the University of Wisconsin - Madison.

The developers of the vignettes and IFSPs were asked to demonstrate the diversity of children and families who are receiving early intervention services. For this reason, the vignettes and service plans are deliberately different from each other in approach. Some vignettes refer to family members by their first names. Others use the more formal Mr., Mrs., or Ms. These and other differences are intentional and reflect the variety of family and program preferences that are part of the IFSP process.

It may be helpful to refer back to these vignettes as the reader encounters the examples and the sample Individualized Family Service Plans.

Vignette #1 -- The Crowder Family

Theresa and Michael Crowder and their three children, Julie, 16; Roger, 7; and Mary, 21 months, live in metropolitan Boston. Mrs. Crowder has AIDS and her youngest child, Mary, who was HIV positive at birth, has recently been diagnosed with AIDS as well. Mrs. Crowder and her husband are separated, and Mrs. Crowder receives Aid to Families with Dependent Children. Mrs. Crowder, Julie, and Mary live in a large subsidized apartment complex.

Mrs. Crowder and her sister Yvonne are very close, and Yvonne is a strong and consistent support to Mrs. Crowder and her children. As Mrs. Crowder's disease has progressed, Yvonne has helped out by having Roger live with her family. Yvonne and her husband run a small corner grocery store in a nearby neighborhood. They have a son a year older than Roger, and the boys are good friends. Whenever Mrs. Crowder is hospitalized for treatment, Yvonne also cares for Julie and Mary in her home. Mrs. and Mr. Crowder have lived separately for the last year. Theresa is struggling to control her drug addiction. Because Mr. Crowder is an active drug user, Mrs. Crowder chooses to live apart from him. She has entered Methadone treatment programs several times in the past two years.

Yvonne has been very supportive of Mrs. Crowder's efforts to manage her addiction, but Yvonne, who has very strong religious beliefs, becomes angry with her sister when she quits treatment. Because she counts on Yvonne for support, Mrs. Crowder has recently promised her sister to recommit to a treatment program. She knows it will be a struggle, but her relationship with Yvonne is very important to her.

Mrs. Crowder's health has begun to fail in the past six months. She battles minor infections and bouts of overwhelming fatigue. Because of her own physical needs, Mrs. Crowder often feels overwhelmed by the demands of her toddler Mary. Julie is a big help to her mother in taking care of Mary.

Although Mrs. Crowder wants Mary to be with other children, she lacks the stamina to take her to the playground or to get together with other mothers and children. She is also very concerned about her neighbors discovering that she and Mary are HIV positive. Mrs. Crowder is very guarded about this medical information and has told no one outside her immediate family. Although she feels very alone, she is frightened of people learning about her disease.

Mary's health is poor. She has chronic diarrhea and recurrent ear infections. Mrs. Crowder says Mary is irritable and hard to comfort. Mary is also quite small for her age, and Mrs. Crowder worries about her daughter's ability to fight infection. Mrs. Crowder mentions mealtimes as particularly stressful for the family. Mary is a fussy eater, often refusing what is offered, and throwing her food on the floor. Mrs. Crowder says that she sometimes feels angry at the baby for making such a mess. Usually, though, she just feels tired at the thought of cleaning it up and is anxious for Mary to become a better eater and get stronger.

Mrs. Crowder was referred to Project WIN, an early intervention program for families with children who are HIV positive, by the social worker at the hospital where she is receiving medical treatment. The social worker has been involved with Mrs. Crowder since Mary was born with neonatal abstinence syndrome, sudden withdrawal of her mother's drugs from her body when she was born. She is concerned that Mrs. Crowder's deteriorating physical condition may make her unable to continue to care for Mary. The social worker has also expressed concern about Mary's developmental status and asked that an assessment be conducted. The hospital social worker was with Mrs. Crowder during her first visit with the early intervention program and accompanied Mrs. Crowder, her two daughters, and her sister to the assessment.

Vignette #2 -- The Griffin Family

Benjamin was born at 26 weeks gestation to Michael and Leslie Griffin. Their daughter, Caroline, was two and a half years old when Ben was born. The Griffins live in Mountain, a rural community in a Western state, an hour away from Medical Center Hospital where Ben spent his first six months of life.

The length of Ben's hospitalization placed a great strain on the Griffin family. Daily two hour trips to the hospital, long absences from Caroline, and continuing concerns over Ben's diagnosis and prognosis have been especially difficult. Further, Leslie, who was working as a guidance counselor when Ben was born, has had to quit her job in order to provide the special care that the baby needs. Leslie regrets having to stop work and says that she misses the sense of purpose and accomplishment that her job provided. It is also hard for the Griffins to lose their second income, particularly at a time when Ben's medical expenses are so great.

Benjamin's medical conditions include Bronchopulmonary Dysplasia (BPD) and a severe cerebral hemorrhage. A comprehensive developmental assessment done while Ben was in the NICU indicated that he would need help with several areas of development. The initial IFSP was written when Ben was five months old, about a month before Ben's tentative discharge date.

When Ben was discharged, he still needed oxygen and was placed on an apnea monitor. The suggestions provided by the NICU physicians helped the Griffins understand Ben's periodic breathing difficulties. Weekly appointments with an occupational therapist and a physical therapist, as well as monthly visits to the pulmonary clinic were scheduled as part of the IFSP.

Fortunately, there is an early intervention program in the Griffins' community. The early childhood special educator from the program visits the Griffins weekly and helps them implement the recommendations of the occupational therapist and the physical therapist, as well as suggesting ways to enhance Benjamin's cognitive development.

The link to the early childhood educator is an important one for the Griffins, although a weekly visit does not give Leslie the support she says she needs, given the amount of extra care that Benjamin requires. Leslie and Michael are familiar with all the therapies designed for Benjamin. They have thought of creative ways to make the therapies a part of their everyday life, but they do not want to be solely responsible for implementing them. Leslie wants very much to be able to assume other roles again, in addition to that of being Ben's mother.

The location of the Griffins' community, which has always been a source of pleasure, has now become a major source of stress. Not only is the hospital where Ben receives his treatment an hour away from their home, it is extremely hard for them to find the kind of support services they need to care for Benjamin in their own community. Access to respite care, equipment vendors, and skilled nursing care is extremely limited.

As they look to the future, the Griffins recognize that there is no preschool program for children with special health needs in their community. The Griffins have developed a large network of friends during their years in Mountain, and leaving the community would be a major disruption for the family. The demands created by Ben's care, however, are causing Leslie and Michael to consider a move.

Vignette #3 -- The Lain Family

Jennifer Owles was born weighing six pounds, six ounces, following a normal pregnancy and delivery. Although she had a low body temperature and poor feeding on admission to the nursery, Jennifer was discharged after two days.

Jennifer and her mother, Ms. Barbara Owles, lived with Barbara's aunt for the first few months after Jenny's birth. Ms. Owles, who is seventeen, works at the neighborhood Burger Palace and, therefore, is unable to care for Jenny during the day. Because Ms. Owles' aunt has four young children of her own to care for, Jenny's daily care was provided by a close friend and neighbor, Olivia Lain, who is also Jenny's godmother.

When Jennifer was two months old, she was admitted to the local emergency room with a temperature of 106.6. She had a grand mal seizure, developed irregular respiration, and was intubated with 100% oxygen. She was transferred by helicopter to Children's Hospital in a nearby city, and required cardiac compression during transport. At Children's Hospital, she suffered multiple seizures and septic shock. She was subsequently placed in a phenobarbital coma while being maintained on a ventilator.

Jennifer was diagnosed with viral encephalitis with resulting neuronal damage and probable subcortical changes. The physician caring for Jennifer at the hospital had a number of concerns about her development: hypotonicity, poor head control, developmental delay, poor vision, and poor interaction with her environment. She referred Jenny and her mother to the local health department for continuing health care and monitoring of the anticonvulsant drugs that Jenny was taking, and she recommended that the health department refer Jennifer to the community-based early intervention program.

Following Jennifer's discharge from Children's Hospital, Olivia Lain became even more involved in Jennifer's care. Jenny began living with Ms. Lain full time when she was six months old. Ms. Lain has taken responsibility for coordinating Jenny's medical management and has worked with the medical team to find the proper levels of seizure medication for Jenny. After the most recent medication change, Jenny is more alert and responsive, and her seizure activity has diminished.

Ms. Lain, with full support from Jenny's mother, has been involved with the early intervention program. As Jenny's seizure medication has been decreased, her developmental progress has improved. Ms. Lain is delighted with Jenny's progress and feels that Jenny has become a real part of her family. Ms. Lain and Jenny's mother have talked with the Social Service Department about Ms. Lain's assuming legal custody of Jenny, with plans to adopt her. Ms. Lain is delighted with the prospect, but from time to time has expressed a concern that Ms. Owles might want to regain custody if Jennifer's progress continues.

Vignette #4 -- The Mack Family

Lita was born at 28 weeks gestation to Mark and Dee Mack. Lita was the Macks' second child -- her older brother, Jeremy, was two years old when she was born. The Mack's live in south central Wisconsin in a rural community about forty minutes from the medical center where Lita was born.

Lita's early life was spent in an isolette in the NICU. Lita was diagnosed as having Bronchopulmonary Dysplasia and a small ventricular septal defect. She spent four months in the hospital and was discharged while she was still on oxygen and an apnea monitor and still fed with a naso-gastric tube. Shortly after Lita was discharged, she was referred to the Linking Infants and Families Together (LIFT) project and was seen by an infant specialist.

One of the Macks' major concerns was Lita's inability to sustain nourishment. Her feeding problems and frequent vomiting bouts resulted in very poor growth. Lita was frequently hospitalized -- trips to the medical center became an almost weekly routine. Dee was left with no time alone and little time to spend with Jeremy.

The Macks were fortunate to have Project LIFT, an early intervention program, in their community. Initially, an early childhood educator and an occupational therapist visited Lita and the Macks. Because Lita's main needs were in the areas of feeding and motor development, the occupational therapist acted as the case coordinator for the Macks. After a speech and language therapist joined the LIFT staff, she shared case coordination responsibilities with the occupational therapist.

Dee was happy with the services that Lita was receiving from LIFT, but she identified other needs that the family had, particularly for respite care and nursing services for Lita. Family finances were not adequate for these needs. Dee also wanted to have some time with Jeremy away from home to meet his growing need for attention. Dee asked for help from Project LIFT, because she had no close friends or family she felt she could turn to for support. Although Dee's sister was supportive when Lita was first released from the hospital, for the most part, Dee and Mark were on their own when it came to taking care of Lita.

Building Positive Relationships Between Professionals and Families

By Donald B. Bailey

True collaboration requires that programs move beyond token representation of families in planning and evaluating services.

Introduction

This chapter is based on the belief that early intervention is a service that "takes place in the relationship and interactions between families . . . and professionals" (Healy et al., 1989, p. 120). Quality interactions between families and professionals are essential if Individualized Family Service Plans are to meet the needs of children and families. This chapter is also an explicit affirmation that the establishment of positive relationships between families and professionals is a worthy goal in and of itself. As one parent of an infant with Down syndrome said, "If you have a written IFSP but had to go through hell to get it, what does that say about the professionals and systems that exist to serve families?"

The success of the IFSP process greatly depends on the communication skills of the professionals involved. The purpose of communication between families and professionals is to exchange, gather, and interpret information in order for families to have the information and support they need to make informed decisions about services for their child and themselves.

Communication between families and professionals can be difficult. Family members and professionals, alike, come from cultural backgrounds that shape their values, beliefs, attitudes, verbal and nonverbal behaviors, and perceptions. Even if these cultural backgrounds are similar, each person is shaped by individual experiences and degrees of acculturation. Furthermore, families and professionals are communicating for a specific purpose, and the very nature of that purpose may influence initial communications due to anxiety, preconceptions, misconceptions, or differing viewpoints and values.

The following scenario from the WINGS Project at the University of Wisconsin - Madison illustrates the need for effective communication skills:

> When Jamie Thunder was two and a half years old, Dr. Johnson, the contract physician at the tribal health clinic, noticed that Jamie had chronic otitis media, his speech was delayed, he was shorter than average, and he had epicanthal folds. Concerned about possible fetal alcohol syndrome, Dr. Johnson made an appointment for Jamie with the regional developmental disabilities center.
>
> No one came to the appointment Dr. Johnson made for the Thunders. Because Jamie was being referred to the center's genetics clinic for possible fetal alcohol syndrome, the center staff wondered if the Thunders were unconcerned about Jamie's health

and development or even uncaring -- perhaps Mrs. Thunder had a drinking problem that interfered with her ability to care for Jamie. The secretary called the Thunders and made another appointment.

Jamie's maternal grandmother, Agnes Browndeer, brought him to this second appointment. Noticing the referral for possible fetal alcohol syndrome, Susan Field, the social work intern who was assigned to do intakes at the center, wanted to interview Jamie's parents and asked Mrs. Browndeer where the Thunders were. Mrs. Browndeer said that Jamie's parents asked her to bring Jamie to the appointment. Mrs. Browndeer also said that neither she nor Jamie's parents knew why Jamie had been referred to the center.

As Susan began to ask the questions on the social history protocol, Mrs. Browndeer became more uncomfortable and the conversation became increasingly stiff and formal. Mrs. Browndeer and the intern seemed to be talking at cross purposes.

Fortunately, George Davies, the center's social work supervisor, was observing the interview and decided to intervene. He joined the conversation, mentioning that he had spent some time on the reservation during his internship. He said he had enjoyed the warmth and hospitality of the tribe. He showed Mrs. Browndeer his watch band, decorated with colorful beadwork, which he said was made by Loraine Taylor. Mrs. Browndeer responded with a smile that Loraine was her cousin -- they had grown up in the same house.

As he talked with Mrs. Browndeer, George Davies learned that transportation to the Center was difficult for the family, because the reservation was 275 miles away and because Lance, Jamie's father, had to use the family's only car to get to his job, which was 30 miles from their community. He also learned that Jamie's mother, Mary, had a half-time job working for the tribal government.

Mrs. Browndeer cared for Jamie while Mary worked. She told George that, like many grandmothers in their tribe, she often makes the first contacts and visits for the family with outside agencies, particularly when her grandchildren are involved.

George was able to assure Mrs. Browndeer that the center's geneticist staffed an outreach clinic once a month in a town much closer to the reservation. He talked over possible appointment times with Mrs. Browndeer and promised to find a time when Jamie's parents could come as well.

Lance and Mary Thunder accompanied Agnes Browndeer and Jamie to the appointment with the geneticist, Dr. Cantrell. Dr. Cantrell found that the Thunders and Mrs. Browndeer were warmly responsive to Jamie and seemed to take equal delight and responsibility in caring for him. He also learned that Lance was "traditional" and was to be inducted into a medicine lodge in the near future.

Lance said that the Creator had given them Jamie as a gift to be cared for tenderly, regardless of any problem that might arise. Dr. Cantrell showed interest in the tribal traditions, and asked if non-Indians were invited to the annual Pow-wow. He learned from Mary that she had not had any alcohol after finding out she was pregnant. Mary said she felt guilty and sad because she remembered drinking some beer just before she learned she was pregnant.

Dr. Cantrell discovered that Lance had a unilateral hearing loss and a perforated eardrum. He also observed that Lance had epicanthal folds, and after further questioning, decided that it was a family trait. After a thorough examination of Jamie, Dr. Cantrell was able to assure Mary that Jamie did not have fetal alcohol syndrome and that his speech delay was probably a result of his history of ear infections. He asked if he could contact their county social services agency,

> which had an early intervention program, to work with the Thunders and Mrs. Browndeer on some ideas for helping Jamie's language development. (D. Jones, personal communication, March 1991)

As this example illustrates, preconceived notions, stereotypes, and assumptions can get in the way of effective communication between families and professionals.

Families and professionals interact throughout the process of seeking, planning, accessing, and evaluating services and resources. The nature and quality of these interactions determine whether or not trusting and supportive partnerships are established between families and professionals. They also provide the context for exchanging the information necessary for informed and shared decision making. Appendix B includes a checklist to promote shared responsibility and collaboration between families and professionals.

Table 3
Elements of Collaboration

- Mutual respect for skills and knowledge
- Honest and clear communication
- Understanding and empathy
- Mutually agreed upon goals
- Shared planning and decision making
- Open and 2-way sharing of information
- Accessibility and responsiveness
- Joint evaluation of progress
- Absence of labeling and blaming

Source: *Focal Point*, (1987), Vol. 2, No. 2, Research and Training Center, Regional Research Institute for Human Services, Portland State University.

Quality Interpersonal Interactions

Quality interpersonal interactions are difficult to describe because they vary considerably with family styles, professional styles, and the way in which they interact. Ultimately, quality of communication is evidenced by the results of the exchange. Among the many characteristics of good interpersonal interactions between families and professionals are those in which families know that professionals:

- actively listen to them;
- treat them with respect and dignity;
- recognize and affirm family values, customs, and beliefs;
- communicate with them openly and honestly;
- provide them with complete and unbiased information about their children;
- build on their strengths;
- acknowledge and address their concerns and needs;
- provide services based on the desires and preferences they communicated and the needs they identified;
- honor their choices; and,
- assist in a process that is beneficial to their children and themselves.

From a family's perspective, quality interpersonal interactions are important for at least three reasons. First, they are more likely to be enjoyable rather than stressful experiences. Second, they serve to reinforce family members' feelings of competence and sense of worth as individuals whose opinions are valued and respected. Finally, they are more likely to result in services based on family priorities and, therefore, in the achievement of IFSP outcomes.

From a professional's perspective, an emphasis on quality interpersonal interactions also has important benefits. By explicitly stating that the development of trusting, warm, and collaborative relationships with families is an important professional goal, professionals may feel that they now have permission to take the time necessary to earn this trust and to develop these relationships. It also is likely that establishing quality relationships with families will provide professionals a greater sense of meaning and accomplishment in their work.

Finally, research in many fields has documented the practical importance of establishing open, positive, and collaborative relationships. Project Dakota, Inc., in Minnesota, formerly a early intervention program and now an outreach training project, changed their model from staff-directed to family-centered. In the process, they shifted staff roles from service provider to consultant, focusing on collaboration and negotiation between families and staff.

As a result of this shift in emphasis, Project Dakota demonstrated a corresponding increase in the number of contributions by families to the entire program planning process. Their data show that parents were the source of 60% of the total contributions to the process. The data also demonstrate that when staff contribute more of the outcomes and strategies to the service plan, parents follow through with only half of the strategies they planned to use; but when parents contribute at least equally to the plan, implementation by parents is 80% to 100% (Kovach, 1986). Thus, quality interpersonal processes and commitment to partnerships are important for reasons of both quality and effectiveness.

How can quality interpersonal processes be incorporated into the IFSP process? At least four components must be in place:

- negotiation and definition of roles and relationships;
- individual relationship-building skills;
- organizational support; and,
- a system that encourages quality interactions at all levels.

The remainder of this chapter addresses each of these key components.

Roles and Relationships

Teachers and therapists in traditional education settings generally view themselves as "experts," whose primary role is to take charge of designing and providing interventions for children. Unfortunately, this model often has been used by early intervention professionals in their work with families. Research, theory, and family opinions, however, suggest that this traditional approach is not generally applicable to work with families. Rather, best practice in early intervention today views families as voluntary consumers of services -- consumers able to choose their level of involvement, the roles they wish to assume, and the services they want to receive.

This perspective often is difficult for professionals to adopt. As one therapist observed, "I entered my field to work with children, not with families." Others have expressed reservations about families having too much control over decision making, feeling that relinquishing control diminishes the value of professional expertise and experience. It is interesting to note, however, that a major trend in marital and family therapy is toward client determination of goals and treatment. As Cecchin (1987) noted:

> As family therapists, we cannot invent a family. What we do best is the bringing forth of patterns through interacting with a family. We cannot think of ourselves as teachers instructing families in better scripts for being families . . . Because we do not know what specific script will be successful for a specific family, we are left to interact in a way . . . that it finds its own new (or rewritten) script. (p. 408)

Thus, the field of family therapy has evolved in the direction that solutions must fit families, rather than being imposed on them. If professionals whose

Principles Underlying Professional Practice

- Children and families may have multiple and diverse needs and, thus, may have to draw on the resources of multiple disciplines and programs. Therefore, a team approach is necessary.
- The team should consist of family members and service providers. Membership will vary depending on family preferences, family strengths and needs, child needs, and agency constraints.
- Families have the right to know all role options and to choose their level of involvement on the team, including serving as team leaders if they so choose.
- Final decisions and approval of the plan rest with the family.
- A family-centered IFSP process does not indicate a passive role for professionals. The responsibility of professionals to openly and honestly share their knowledge, opinions, and concerns remains unchanged.

training has been specifically focused on families are taking such an approach, it would seem even more important for early intervention professionals, whose training has been primarily child-focused, to adopt a similar approach.

In recent years, many early intervention professionals have begun to compare their role with families to that of consultants who are hired to provide expert opinions and who make recommendations, but *not* final decisions (Kjerland & Kovach, 1987; Leviton, Mueller, & Kauffman, 1991). The consultant model provides a balance between a professional's disciplinary expertise and a family's decision-making authority and responsibility for its child and itself.

In negotiating and defining roles and relationships, the following principles should underlie professional practice:

- Children and families may have multiple and diverse needs and may need to draw on the resources of a variety of disciplines and programs. Therefore, a team approach to services is necessary.
- The team should consist of family members and service providers. Membership will vary depending on family preferences; family concerns, resources, and priorities; child needs; and agency constraints.
- Families have the right to know all role options and to choose their level of involvement on the team, including serving as team leaders if they so choose.
- Final decisions and approval of the plan rest with the family.
- A family-centered IFSP process does not indicate a passive role for professionals. The responsibility of professionals to openly and honestly share their knowledge, opinions, and concerns remains unchanged.

Interpersonal Skills Needed by Professionals

Professionals need several key skills to respond to families as consumers and to fill the role of family consultant and advocate. Among these are the following:

- a family-centered philosophical approach;
- effective communication skills; and
- skills related to team process and decision making.

These skills are described in greater detail in the following pages.

Family-Centered Approach

Many models have been offered to describe family development, organization, and functioning. To expect professionals to adopt a common theoretical model for their work with families is unrealistic. All professionals, however, should recognize that families are complex and interactive systems, with their own established values, structures, and functions (Aponte, 1986).

Each family has an identified set of tasks or functions, such as earning money or caring for children. Families establish their own structures and interaction patterns within which these functions are accomplished. These structures are embedded within the values that families have consciously or unconsciously adopted. For example, some families adopt a traditional approach to domestic tasks in which these tasks are the mother's primary responsibility, whereas other families decide that these tasks are to be shared.

Professionals must recognize that the values, structures, and interaction patterns of families are part of their very being -- they help define who they are as a family. When professionals ask families to change their values, structures, or interaction patterns in ways that seem appropriate to the professional but that are inconsistent with family values and preferences, the inevitable result is conflict. Such conflict may result in a negative family/professional relationship, a lack of family follow-through on commitments, or a family's withdrawal from a program or service.

Focusing on functional outcomes that are important to a family ensures that family structures, values, and interaction patterns will be respected and accepted by the professionals on the IFSP team. In fact, the development of functional IFSP outcomes can be "a mechanism for clarifying the relationship between professionals and families and the expectations for that relationship" (Bailey, 1988, p. 233).

For example:

Vignette #1 -- In talking about her priorities for the IFSP, Mrs. Crowder said that she wants to control her drug addiction so that she can maintain her relationship with her sister, who she depends on for help in the care of her toddler with AIDS and her other children. As one of the outcomes and corresponding activities in her IFSP, Mrs. Crowder and the rest of the team included controlling her drug addiction by entering a drug treatment program.

When Mrs. Crowder brought up this issue with the team and asked for this outcome, she invited them into a private part of her life, and helped define her relationship with the early intervention program and her primary service provider. As part of this process, their expectations of each other in this particular area were clarified and made explicit -- Mrs. Crowder would tell her primary service provider when she felt like using drugs, and the service provider would tell Mrs. Crowder when she thought Mrs. Crowder was using drugs.

Table 4
Professional Checklist

- Do I really believe that parents are my equal and, in fact, are experts on their child?
- Do I show the same respect for the value of parents' time as I do for my own time by educating myself about an individual child before appointments or group sessions?
- Do I speak plainly and avoid medical, psychological, or social work jargon?
- Do I make appointments and provide services at times and places that are convenient for the family?
- Do I share information with other professionals to insure both that services are not duplicated and that families do not expend unnecessary energy searching for providers and services?

Source: Adapted from *Focal Point*, (1987), Vol. 2, No. 2, Research and Training Center, Regional Research Institute for Human Services, Portland State University, Adapted from Alexander, R. and Tompkins-McGill, P. (1987). Notes to the experts from the parent of a handicapped child. *Social Work*, 32(4), 361-362.

Conflicts between families and professionals can occur in any family/professional relationship. It is important for professionals to try to understand life from the family's perspective or perspectives, without making judgments. By seeking to understand the way in which individual families interpret events, set priorities, and make decisions, professionals are more likely to establish trusting and collaborative relationships with families, and services are more likely to be consistent with family preferences and needs.

Effective Communication Skills

Building trusting relationships with families entails more than a simple acceptance that doing so is a good idea. Changes in staff attitudes are not enough -- professionals must develop new skills and practices as well, in order to establish quality interactions and partnerships with families (Kjerland & Kovach, 1987).

Quality interpersonal processes are built on effective communication skills (Winton, 1988; Winton & Bailey, 1988). These skills include listening, as well as sending messages. One of the most frequent complaints of parents is that professionals do not listen to them. Professionals often feel that they need to jump in and offer explanations or solutions to problems. Although problem-solving is an important skill, if done too early it can be counterproductive, especially if families feel that professionals are offering solutions without adequate information.

When asked to describe professional behaviors that are most helpful, one rural family related the following experience:

> A public health nurse came to our house to talk about our infant son, who has special needs. When she came in, she asked us "How can I help you?" Then she *really* listened. She listened to us talk for over two hours before she made a single suggestion. You don't know what a relief that was after all the other professionals who start telling us how we can solve our problems before they know anything about our family and what we want for our son and ourselves.

In addition to listening, at least three other communication skills enhance family/professional relationships: reflecting feelings; reflecting content; and effective questioning (Winton, 1988). *Reflecting feelings* refers to a professional's ability to identify and reflect upon how a family member feels about a particular topic. Reflection of feelings requires: "(a) the ability to perceive a person's inner feelings accurately and sensitively and (b) the ability to communicate understanding of those feelings in appropriate language" (Winton & Bailey, 1988, p. 202).

Reflecting content refers to a professional's ability to understand the content of a family member's communication. Reflecting content means: "(a) paraphrasing the main idea of a family member's message and (b) recapitulating and summarizing what has been said" (Winton & Bailey, 1988, p. 203).

Effective questioning and interviewing refers to the ability to ask questions in a way that shares information. Winton and Bailey (1988) recommended the use of both open-ended and close-ended questions, as well as other techniques -- such as expectant facial expressions, head nods, and the use of silence -- that convey to a family the message "Tell me more." Certain questioning skills are also effective in helping family members generate goals, strategies for meeting these goals, and criteria for success (Tomm, 1987).

Professionals also need to communicate in ways that are clear, jargon-free, respectful, and honest. Such communication is the foundation of collaboration and partnerships between families and professionals and among professionals from different disciplines.

Interacting on a Team

The ability to participate effectively on an interdisciplinary team is a key skill for professionals. A variety of team models are used in early intervention. In recent years, those team models that emphasize communication and interaction among team members and the family's role as decision maker on the team have been gaining increasing attention

Table 5
Parent Checklist

- Do I believe I am an equal partner with professionals, and accept my share of the responsibility for solving problems and making plans on behalf of my child?
- Do I clearly express my own needs and the needs of my family to professionals in an assertive manner?
- Do I treat each professional as an individual and avoid letting past negative experiences or negative attitudes get in the way of establishing a good working relationship?
- Do I communicate quickly with professionals serving my child when significant changes or notable events occur?
- When I make a commitment to a professional for a plan of action, do I follow through and complete that commitment?
- Do I maintain realistic expectations of professionals, myself, and my child?

Source: *Focal Point*, (1987), Vol. 2, No. 2, Research and Training Center, Regional Research Institute for Human Services, Portland State University.

(Fewell, 1983; Linder, 1987; Peterson, 1987). In particular, there has been much discussion of communication problems on teams made up of members from multiple disciplines (Bailey, 1984; Blechert, Christiannsen, & Kari, 1987; Woodruff & McGonigel, 1988). Howard (1982) lists five characteristics necessary for effective participation on an interdisciplinary team:

> an atmosphere of (a) acceptance of differences in skills; (b) acceptance of differences in approach; (c) willingness not to try to know everything; (d) an ability to call on others for assistance and ongoing knowledge; and (e) non-threatening opportunities for discussion in these areas. (p. 320)

An equally important professional skill is the ability to facilitate a family's chosen role on the team. Parents frequently report feeling threatened and uncomfortable in interdisciplinary team meetings. Perhaps this is an inevitable consequence of such meetings, in which such emotion-laden issues as diagnosis, placement, or services are often addressed. Furthermore, the presence of several professionals can be intimidating for many parents. This is particularly likely in early intervention programs, since most families with very young children are not likely to have had prior experience in such meetings.

In recent years, family-centered early intervention programs, parent-to-parent organizations, and others have been working to develop policies and practices that facilitate the family's role as primary decision maker on the early intervention team. At the policy level, parent/professional collaboration in program planning, development, and evaluation helps ensure family-centered services. True collaboration requires that programs move beyond token representation of parents in the planning and evaluation of services. Many programs are establishing parent advisory committees or ensuring that existing advisory groups include at least half parent membership.

At the level of services for an individual child and family, a number of practices have been proven effective in facilitating a family's role in the team process. Among them are the following practices:

- Team meetings belong to families and professionals together. Therefore, families, like all other team members, are always made aware of why a meeting is being held, who will be there, and what to expect.
- Families are invited to speak first in team meetings -- to give their perspectives and describe their observations *before* staff give theirs.
- Any medical, technical, or disciplinary-specific terms that are used by staff are *automatically* explained or defined in everyday language, *every* time they are used, until all team members are comfortable with the terms.

- When staff are uncertain about any fact or piece of information, they tell families so. "I am not sure" and "I don't know" are expressions that many families say they appreciate hearing from professionals.

- When professional members of the team disagree about any aspect of assessment or programming, they are open with families and with each other about the differences in opinion or perspective.

- Professionals speak of a family in the same manner, whether or not the family is present. In other words, if a professional staff member is unwilling to address an issue with the family, he or she does not discuss the issue with other staff.

Organizational Support for Interpersonal Processes

Basic communication skills and quality interpersonal interactions between families and professionals are important at all times. Organizational constraints on staff time and other resources, however, often make it difficult for such interactions to occur. At least four types of organizational support are needed:

1. Organizations (e.g., agencies, programs, and their administrators) need to be aware of the critical importance of establishing positive relationships between parents and professionals and should openly communicate that importance to staff members. Unfortunately, the relationship between families and schools for older children has often been characterized as adversarial. Establishing an advocacy-oriented perspective will be difficult in some early intervention programs. Explicit organizational endorsement of the importance of positive, collaborative relationships between families and professionals is essential if they are to be implemented.

2. Organizations must provide the resources that make quality interpersonal interactions possible. *The single most important resource is time.* Quality interactions simply cannot be rushed. Although time is a real and tangible cost for early intervention programs, an early investment of time in earning a family's trust and building an open relationship can result in much time saved when interactions that are more formal, less direct, and more guarded are short-circuited over the course of the relationship. Such an early time investment is also likely to result in a higher percentage of outcomes attained and greater consumer satisfaction.

3. Organizations must provide adequate training and supervision. Many professionals have had very little training in working with families and other adults. Effective communication skills must be practiced continually in order to be maintained. Families and professionals have much to offer each other in collaborative side-by-side training. Families can be invited to participate in all stages of staff inservice from planning to implementation and in any role in which they are interested and comfortable, from trainer to learner.

4. An evaluation of the process by which the IFSP is developed and implemented should be a part of a program's overall evaluation plan. Typically, program evaluation efforts have focused on child-related outcomes (e.g., Did children make developmental progress, achieve objectives, improve behavior?). As this chapter has emphasized, when working with families, the process by which outcomes are developed and achieved is as important as the outcomes themselves. Thus, assessment of factors such as parent satisfaction, family participation, and family independence in decision making should be a basic component of program evaluation efforts.

Creating a System that Works

In order to ensure that quality interactions occur at all levels, a system that facilitates these interactions across agencies must be in place. Given the inevitability of multiple agency involvement in the provision of early intervention services, cross-agency, or transagency, collaboration is essential.

Similar collaboration is necessary among professionals in private practice and agencies involved in early intervention services. Often, an early intervention program can assist by encouraging frequent communication between, for example, the child's pediatrician and the therapists employed by the program.

Professionals and agencies also should encourage noninvolved agencies to become aware of the ways in which they, too, can be of help to families whose young children have special needs. Furthermore, policy-makers at all levels must be convinced that such activities are a legitimate and necessary part of the process of serving young children and their families.

It won't be easy to create a system that works; yet families and professionals across the country are making great strides as they work together to implement Part H. Healy and colleagues (1989) described the challenge this way:

> The Law cannot by itself carry out a revolution in service practices. The concepts of meaningful collaboration between families and professionals, and of true family-centeredness in services are still, in practice, revolutionary concepts. There is a world of difference between talking about parent empowerment and making it a reality. The barriers that have existed to this shift from talk to practice will not be overcome by the law alone. To make the most important parts of this law a reality, it will take creativity and vision, as well as the continued vigilance of parents and other advocates who have been so central to the establishment of these principles. (p. 121)

Identifying Children's Strengths and Needs

By Ann P. Turnbull

The key to family-centered assessment is that individual preferences be identified and respected and that families participate in the process according to what they feel is right for them.

Introduction

Like the IFSP process itself, assessment is nonlinear, interactive exchange that is shaped by families' priorities for themselves and their children. This chapter describes a flexible, evolving, family-centered process for child assessment as part of the IFSP process. It does not attempt to provide a cookbook of assessment instruments or techniques. There are no magical instruments or questionnaires that can substitute for authentic understanding born of lengthy acquaintance, mutual trust, and rapport.

Principles

The principles that should guide assessment evolve from the family-centered philosophy and conceptual framework described in Chapter Two. These principles are as follows:

- **Assessment is a continuing, evolving process rather than a discrete activity that can be initiated and completed at a single point in time.**

It is impossible to get a complete understanding of a child's strengths and needs from a single assessment point or even several points. Dynamic, evolutionary assessment requires continuous opportunities for gathering, exchanging, and interpreting information. Continuing assessment is also necessary because a child's strengths and needs are in a constant state of change in infancy and early childhood.

- **Child assessment should be shaped by family priorities and information needs, as well as by child characteristics and diagnostic concerns.**

Traditionally, families' priorities for themselves and their children were not identified until after an assessment was completed. Most often, the same assessment process, instruments, and procedures were used for all children and families, with relatively minor adaptations made depending on the kind or severity of the child's disability. Family questions or concerns typically played little part in shaping the assessment, so that the process and findings often met the needs of the staff and program, rather than the needs of the family. By determining the content of the assessment, professionals also shaped the content of the service plan.

Many early intervention programs, however, are changing this practice. Beginning with the first contacts with a family and continuing throughout assessment, identification of family resources and concerns, outcome development, and IFSP evaluation, a family is asked to share its agenda for the child and family -- the family priorities that will shape the entire IFSP process and ultimately determine the IFSP outcomes.

If the assessment is to be accurate and complete and if family members are to have the information they need to be informed decision makers, then professionals are obliged to share concerns they have about a child that a family may not have identified. For example, a pediatrician concerned about a baby's pallor, listlessness, and high likelihood of anemia will share these observations with the family so that they can plan together for intervention.

- **Informed consent must be obtained from parents or guardians for any and all assessment activities.**

No assessment of an infant or toddler can take place without the informed, written consent of the child's parent(s) or legal guardian(s). Covert observations or assessments should not be used unless there is an imperative need to do so and unless the parent(s) or guardian(s) have given explicit permission for such procedures.

- **The assessment process must reflect a respect for family values and styles of decision making.**

Families differ widely in the degree to which they wish to participate, both in the assessment process and in other parts of an early intervention program. This is a choice that families must make for themselves. It is the professionals' responsibility to ensure that families are provided with the information and support necessary for them to make an informed decision on this and other matters. Just as needs change, so, too, do family preferences. A family-centered assessment process is one that changes to keep pace with an individual family's changing preferences.

- **A team process for assessment means that all information should be shared in a give-and-take fashion. Family members of the team should have the opportunity to be present for all discussion.**

Principles Guiding The Assessment Process

- Assessment is a continuing, evolving process rather than a discrete activity that can be initiated and completed at a single point in time.
- Child assessment should be shaped by family priorities and information needs, as well as by child characteristics and diagnostic concerns.
- Informed consent must be obtained from a family for any and all assessment activities.
- The assessment process must reflect a respect for family values and styles of decision making.
- A team process for assessment means that all information should be shared in a give-and-take fashion. Family members of the team should have the opportunity to be present for all discussion.
- Language associated with the assessment process should reflect family preferences as much as possible.

Because families and professionals are partners on the intervention team, it is not appropriate for professional members of the team to meet alone for the purpose of developing consensus on certain assessment results or interpretations. Such a "professionals only" meeting effectively excludes families from meaningful team participation. If it is important to discuss the meaning of assessment results in order to reach agreement, families should be able to participate in those meetings as well as in any meeting where results are interpreted. Unless it is their explicit choice, parents should never be "greeted by a group of professionals who have already huddled, debated, and decided" on the meaning of assessment results (Kjerland & Kovach, 1987, p. 11).

Some families will choose to be present at summary discussions only, while others will choose to be present at all team discussions of their child. In order for families to have this choice, however, team meetings need to be held at times and places that are convenient for the family, and the family must be made fully aware of all opportunities for decision making.

The policy of creating opportunities for families to be present at all decision-making times does not preclude opportunities for staff members to work together without family participation for the purpose of improving their performance or for clinical supervision. During such meetings, the focus is not on an individual child or family, but on the skills and resources staff need to work effectively.

- **Language associated with the assessment process should reflect family preferences as much as possible.**

Family preferences should be used in the selection of terminology used to gather and exchange information about the child. Many families interpret terms such as "evaluation" to mean a process in which their personal competence and their value as a family is being analyzed, critiqued, or questioned. Because of this concern, it may be advisable to use other terms that are more reflective of partnerships between families and staff. It should be noted, however, that the Part H regulations do define the terms "evaluation" and "assessment" (see Table 6); if states choose to use other terminology, they must ensure that their policies and procedures comply with the law and regulations.

The use of family language is more than a semantic issue. Language can be either an aid or a barrier to partnerships. In order to enhance family/professional partnerships, professionals should listen to the terms that families use, ask them directly about the terminology that they prefer, and use those terms whenever possible.

To enable families to participate fully as team members, professional members of the team should avoid using professional jargon. Use of jargon jeopardizes both the clarity and tone of communication between professionals and families.

Table 6
Definition of "Evaluation" and "Assessment"
{34 CFR 300.322}

- Evaluation "means the procedures used by appropriate qualified personnel to determine a child's initial and continuing eligibility under this part . . . including determining the status of the child in each of the developmental areas in paragraph (c)(3)(ii) of this section."

- Assessment "means the ongoing procedures used by appropriate qualified personnel throughout the period of a child's eligibility under this part to identify -- (i) The child's unique needs; (ii) The family's strengths and needs related to development of the child; and (iii) The nature and extent of early intervention services that are needed by the child and the child's family to meet the needs in paragraph (b)(2)(i) and (b)(2)(ii) of this section."

Assessment Planning

To plan an assessment that is tailored to an individual child and family, the team should gather and exchange information in the following areas:

- child characteristics;
- family preferences for involvement;
- family priorities for both the child and family; and
- child records and other data from previous assessments or diagnoses.

Table 7
Pre-Assessment Planning: The Setting

1. What questions or concerns do others have (e.g., babysitter, clinic, preschool)?

2. Are there other places where we should observe your child?

   Place:
   Contact Person:
   What to Observe:

3. How does your child do around other children?

4. Where would you like the assessment to take place?

5. What time of day? (The best time is when your child is alert and when working parents can be present.)

6. Are there others who should be there in addition to parents and staff?

7. What are your child's favorite toys or activities that help him become focused, motivated, and comfortable?

8. Which roles would you find comfortable during assessment?
   ___ a. sit beside your child
   ___ b. help with activities to explore her abilities
   ___ c. offer comfort and support to your child
   ___ d. exchange ideas with the facilitator
   ___ e. carry out activities to explore your child's abilities
   ___ f. prefer facilitator to handle and carry out activities with your child
   ___ g. other

Source: Project Dakota Outreach, Dakota, Inc., Eagan, MN.

The final item in the above list will depend on how much of their previous service history family members would like to share with an early intervention program.

Many model early intervention programs have developed excellent forms and procedures to help staff and family plan a "tailored" assessment. Table 7 is an example of one such questionnaire, developed by Project Dakota, to plan both the process for and content of their tailored assessments. Other sample checklists, forms, and written procedures are provided in Appendix C.

As part of pre-assessment planning, many programs will identify a temporary case manager, or service coordinator, to ensure that the assessment progresses in a smooth, timely, and comfortable manner for the family. Other programs will identify a temporary service coordinator with the family during first contacts. This person could be a physician or nurse from the NICU, a representative from the early intervention program, or any other person who is able to support the family through the assessment process. If the family has a preference for the assignment of a temporary service coordinator, its preference should be respected if possible.

For some families, enough information will have been gathered during their first contacts with a program to plan a tailored assessment. For other families, a formal assessment of the child may be unnecessary because she has recently been assessed by another team, either in the hospital, a regional diagnosis and evaluation center, or another early intervention program. This determination should be made as part of the assessment planning process.

Child Assessment

Child assessment involves several components: (1) identifying and exchanging family perspectives on child strengths and needs; (2) identifying and exchanging professional perspectives on child strengths and needs; and (3) sharing assessment findings and interpreting their meanings. The team may need to meet several times to ensure that the questions and concerns of all team members, especially those of the family, have been addressed.

The particular assessment process chosen by an early intervention program will vary depending on many individual factors. A family-centered approach to assessment, however, requires that families be provided an opportunity to participate in at least the following assessment decisions:

- Which professional disciplines will be involved, and who will be on the assessment team?
- What will be the family's role on the assessment team?
- What kinds of assessment measures will be used?
- When and how will assessment information be synthesized and shared?

Families' priorities and expectations for their children should guide the choice of assessment instruments and should help determine in which domains the assessment will be concentrated. For example, parents may express the hope that their toddler will be able to play in the park with other children. This priority may signal the assessment team to concentrate their efforts on the following areas: (1) the gross motor skills the child needs to use playground equipment; (2) the language skills she needs to communicate at the park; (3) the physical stamina required to actually play; (4) the social skills she needs to play with other children; and (5) the resources the family needs to make everything happen, such as transportation and babysitting for the other children in the family.

Many families will choose to be very actively involved in the assessment process -- being present at all times throughout the assessment, seeking information from other team members, presenting family agendas and concerns, and ensuring that these concerns are addressed. Other families will prefer a less active role, choosing primarily to answer questions from staff about their own goals for their children and themselves (Woodruff & McGonigel, 1988). The key to family-centered assessment is that individual preferences be identified and respected and that families participate in the process according to what they feel is right for them.

Required Assessment Components

Although Part H does not prescribe particular assessment formats or procedures, the statute does require that the IFSP include a "statement of the infant's or toddler's present levels of physical development, cognitive development, language and speech development, psycho-social development, and self-help skills, based on acceptable objective criteria" {1477(d)(1)}. The regulations clarify that physical development includes vision, hearing, and health status {303.344(a)}.

Bailey (1988) recommended the following practices for this component of the IFSP process:

> a. State the child's strengths as well as needs
>
> b. Emphasize functional abilities rather than test scores
>
> c. Place abilities within a developmental context
>
> d. Describe abilities in all relevant developmental domains
>
> e. Include less traditional child-related information such as behavioral characteristics
>
> f. Describe functional limitations of the child (e.g., sensory impairment, motor impairment, chronic health problem) likely to be relevant to intervention planning. (p. 245)

Family Perspectives on Child Strengths and Needs

Hunt and her co-authors (1990) advised other families on the essential nature of the information they have to share about their children:

> You have valuable information and insights about your child that no one else has. You can answer questions that enable people to

> know your child as an individual: his or her dislikes, medical history, personality, and countless other personal characteristics that make you child so rare and wonderful. (p. 11)

Identifying and sharing professional perspectives on a child's strengths and needs is a very familiar activity for early intervention program staff. Most professionals are less familiar, however, with how to elicit and listen to families' perspectives on their children's strengths and needs.

The Family's Assessment Focus (Project Dakota, 1986) can help professionals with this activity. Family members are given the opportunity to talk or write about the child in everyday terms. Items that elicit this kind of information include:

- I would describe my child in this way;
- A typical day with my child includes;
- What my child is really good at or likes to do;
- What my child needs help with or avoids;
- Recent progress or changes I have seen in my child at home; and
- My child is really interested in.

Providing families with the opportunity to think and talk about their children's strengths and needs in this context is likely to be more productive with most families than asking about their children's developmental level or cognitive skills.

Helping families to consider their children's strengths is extremely important. Parents may be consumed with worry about "what's wrong with our baby." Families often say that their family member with a disability has made many positive contributions to their lives, such as strengthening the family, teaching tolerance and patience, giving unconditional love, and giving meaning to life (Turnbull, Guess, & Turnbull, 1989).

Peggy, the grandmother and guardian of LeMar, who is two years old and attends the Family Child Learning Center in Tallemadge, Ohio, shared her insight on this issue:

> There are no magical instruments or questionnaires that can substitute for authentic understanding born of lengthy acquaintance, mutual trust, and rapport.

> When I see LeMar in the classroom, I appreciate who he is and what he's capable of. Some things he does differently, some he doesn't do as well, and some he does better than others. I have gained so much respect for LeMar, and I know now that whatever he does, he'll do it at his own pace, and in his own time.

Methods and Measures

The assessment team can use many different formal and informal measures and methods of gathering information to identify the strengths, needs, and developmental levels of the child. Among the measures are standardized instruments, developmental checklists, observational measures, and checklists completed by family members. A mother of a child in early intervention shared a caution about assessment measures:

> Save us from the document that contains mainly scores from developmental checklists and tests that only enumerate all that our kids can't do and mean such hell to parents!

Assessment measures should be carefully chosen to match child and family characteristics and professional training and expertise. A NEC*TAS-convened Expert Team on child assessment and screening developed a monograph that discusses factors to consider in establishing screening and assessment procedures, *Screening and Assessment: Guidelines for Identifying Young Disabled and Developmentally Vulnerable Children and Their Families* (Meisels & Provence, 1989).

The method used to gather assessment information about the child is as important as the measure. Many written materials and training resources are available to early intervention program teams that are interested in learning more about family-centered assessment methods.

Part H regulations require that assessment methods and measures be nondiscriminatory. Section 303.323 of the regulations specifies that:

- measures and procedures must be administered in the native language or other communication mode of the parents, unless it is clearly not feasible to do so;
- procedures and materials are selected and administered so that they are not "racially or culturally discriminatory";
- no single procedure is used as the sole criterion for determining eligibility; and
- evaluations and assessments are conducted by qualified personnel.

Culturally competent early intervention programs and professionals, however, will go far beyond these minimum requirements to embrace the information gathering traditions and preferences of the communities they serve.

Tips for Discussing Assessment Information with Families

- Discuss information with families as quickly as possible after children's special needs are suspected or formally identified.
- Use the primary language and communication style of the family, and ensure that terminology is clear and understandable.
- Set aside sufficient time for families and professionals to present information, ask questions, and provide emotional support.
- Provide families with an opportunity to decide on the appropriate family members and professionals to include in assessment conferences. Scheduling should allow for the participation of these designated team members.
- Honor family preferences for the amount of information they can absorb in one meeting. Continuing family and professional assessment feedback sessions are necessary, rather than only one or two sessions.
- Provide complete, unbiased information to families about their children's strengths and needs. Throughout the discussion of all information, families need and look for hope and encouragement.

Discussing and Interpreting Results

Traditionally, assessments of the child were conducted by professionals according to their professional disciplines and were followed by a time during which staff synthesized results to share with family members at a later meeting. Best practice in recent years, however, has shifted toward sharing information and results with families as soon as they are gathered. The process of gathering information about the child should be intermingled with the reciprocal process of sharing it.

Project Trans/Team Outreach, an EEPCD project at Child Development Resources in Lightfoot, Virginia, uses an assessment process that prevents staff from interpreting assessment data and making decisions without the family present. The family and the assessment facilitator work with the child, while the other team members observe. Following this transdisciplinary assessment, the entire team meets immediately to discuss their observations and possible interpretations. The family is asked to share their thoughts and observations first. If staff are uncertain about any aspect of what they saw, they share their uncertainty with the family and with each other.

Families can be true team members only when they have access to the same information that other team members use to form opinions and make recommendations. Such information should be presented to families in a clear and unambiguous manner. Often families and professionals have a different understanding of the meaning of commonly used terms. This lack of shared meaning is a frequent cause of communication problems between families and professionals. One father related his experience:

> When they said 'delayed' I thought of all the trains going from New Jersey to New York. Jeff's on a slower train, but he's going to get to New York. They knew all along that he was never going to get to New York. Their 'delay' was my 'off the track.' (Healy et al., 1989, p. 55)

Assessment Timelines

Part H regulations specify that a child's initial evaluation and assessment will be completed within 45 days from the time the responsible public agency receives a referral from a primary referral source {303.321-322}. If exceptional circumstances make it impossible for the 45 day timeline to be met, those circumstances must be documented, and an interim IFSP can be developed and implemented, with the consent of the family {303.322 and 303.345}. This interim IFSP provision is intended to permit provision of immediate services when a child's or family's need is clear from the start; it is not intended as a means to allow programs to circumvent the evaluation and assessment timelines.

Identifying Family Concerns, Priorities, and Resources

By Roxane K. Kaufmann and Mary J. McGonigel

Your identification of resources, strengths, and concerns becomes the foundation of your individual plan -- and no one knows these better than you do. (Hunt, M., et al. (1990). Into our lives *(p. 3). Akron, OH: Children's Hospital Medical Center)*

Introduction

Part H and its accompanying regulations require that the IFSP, with the concurrence of the family, include a statement of the "family's strengths and needs related to enhancing the development of the child" {303.344(b)}. This chapter describes family-centered approaches to this aspect of the IFSP process. Seven principles are outlined and methods and measures are discussed.

From the beginning of the Part H program, families and professionals alike have been concerned about the potential intrusiveness of this activity, which is described variously in both the law and regulations as "family assessment" and "identification of family strengths and needs." Sharing this concern, the IFSP Expert Team and Task Force were unanimous in agreeing not to use the term "family assessment" in the original monograph, but instead to use "identification of family strengths and needs" as a term more in keeping with a family-centered IFSP process.

Since the first edition of the monograph was published, many professionals and families have come to prefer a still more family-centered concept, that of identification of family concerns, priorities, and resources. In this context, both family assessment and identification of family strengths and needs can be defined as:

> the ongoing and interactive process by which [families share and] professionals gather information in order to determine family priorities for goals and services. . . . The primary goal is for professionals to understand what families want for themselves and their children and what they need from professionals in order to achieve those aspirations. In this context, a family need may be viewed as a family's expressed desire for services to be obtained or outcomes to be achieved. A family strength is the family's perceptions of resources that are at its disposal that could be used to meet family needs. (Bailey, in press)

At the heart of a family-centered approach to this part of the IFSP process is the recognition that only a family can determine for itself the concerns, priorities, and resources that it brings to early intervention. In a keynote speech on IFSPs, Lisbeth Vincent (1990) beautifully illustrated this point by describing the experience of one program and family (for purposes of sharing this story, the family can be called the "Silvas"):

Family Concerns: Areas that family members identify as needs, issues, or problems they want to address as part of the IFSP process.

Family Priorities: A family's agenda and choices for how early intervention will be involved in family life.

Family Resources: The strengths, abilities, and formal and informal supports that can be mobilized to meet family concerns, needs, or outcomes.

The Silvas moved to Los Angeles from Central America. The Silva family consisted of the mother and father, the father's brother, and a toddler with Down syndrome. Mr. Silva and his brother were pleased to find work right away as day laborers. The Silvas were connected to an early intervention program very soon after they moved to the city.

The cost of housing in Los Angeles is prohibitive, and in recent years, many newly arrived immigrant families have rented unfinished garages to live in. Mr. Silva found such garage housing for his family. The dedicated and empathetic staff at the early intervention program were concerned that the Silvas were living in substandard housing, with no indoor bathroom, and no insulation. Assuming that the Silvas wanted better housing, the staff began several efforts to find them a better place to live.

After about six weeks of contact with the early intervention program, the Silvas stopped coming to the program. The staff were puzzled and tried to find out what was wrong. They discovered that Mr. Silva had been very proud of the living situation he had provided for his family in the United States. Never before had the Silvas had such a solidly built home and so much privacy. When the early intervention staff assumed the Silvas wanted new housing, they unintentionally projected their values and choices onto the Silva family. Mr. Silva's pride and sense of achievement were hurt in the process, and the family responded by dropping out of the program.

Many early intervention professionals can relate similar experiences in their journey toward family-centered care.

Principles

The principles that should guide the identification of family concerns, priorities, and resources are based on the same family-centered foundation as all other aspects of the IFSP process. These principles are as follows:

- **The inclusion of family information in the IFSP is voluntary on the part of families.**

Part H absolutely does *not* require a family assessment or assessment of the family. The law and regulations are clear that participation in any activity to identify family strengths and needs must be "voluntary on the part of the family," must be "based on information provided by the family," and must "incorporate the family's own description of its strengths and needs relating to enhancing the child's development" {303.322(d)}. Note 1 accompanying regulation 303.344 further emphasizes that the "degree to which the needs of the family are addressed in the IFSP process [is] determined in a collaborative manner with the full agreement and participation of the parents."

- **The identification of family concerns, priorities, and resources is based on an individual family's determination of which aspects of family life are relevant to the child's development.**

The boundaries of this part of the IFSP process should be set by individual families and honored by practitioners. It is not for professionals to determine those areas of family life in which family concerns, resources, and priorities should be identified. Only families can decide for themselves which aspects of family life are relevant to their ability to help their children develop.

Family members should not be asked to provide information about themselves that does not directly relate to their priorities. *As a rule, no information should be collected from families that isn't necessary to provide direct family-centered early intervention services or referral and linkage services.* Assessment of family dynamics, family stress, family relationships, and similar issues cannot be a precondition to a family's participation in services (Dunst, 1988; McGonigel & Garland, 1988).

Families differ in the degree to which they choose to invite an early intervention program into their lives, and the IFSP process should reflect this fact. For example, marital satisfaction should be identified as an area for assessment only if the family (1) identifies marital issues as a barrier to meeting the child's needs, and (2) specifically requests help in this area.

- **A family need or concern exists only if the family perceives that the need or concern exists.**

This principle is one of the most challenging for many early intervention professionals as they shift from their traditional role as expert decision makers to newer roles as consultants to families. Bailey (in press) described this concept of family needs:

> a need exists only if a family member expresses a desire for services to be obtained or outcomes to be achieved. Of course, this does not mean that professionals should hide information or concerns from families. As a rule of thumb, however, this guideline is probably more defensible than overt or covert attempts to "force" families to recognize needs they do not perceive to exist. The likely consequence of such an approach is alienation and distrust on the part of the family.

Such alienation would be fatal to the family/professional collaboration and partnerships that are essential in any family-centered IFSP process.

When Is a Need Really a Need?

In a family-centered IFSP process, "a need exists only if a family member expresses a desire for services to be obtained or outcomes to be achieved" (Bailey, in press).

- **Families have a broad array of formal and informal options to choose from in determining how they will identify their concerns, priorities, and resources.**

Individual families and family members differ in how they prefer to share family information. There is no one right approach for everyone. Some families will choose a more formal or structured approach, such as written surveys or checklists. Others will choose a more informal option, such as chatting with one other member of the IFSP team. As Bailey (in press) described:

> Research and common sense suggest that the issue of interviews versus surveys is not an either-or question. Rather, the issue is which procedure is more useful at a specific time with an individual family and an individual professional for a particular purpose.

Such family preferences must be identified and respected.

- **Families have multiple and continuing opportunities to identify their concerns, priorities, and resources.**

In a family-centered IFSP process, from the moment families first make contact with the early intervention system they begin to shape that process by the questions they ask and the information they choose to share. In this broad sense, every interaction that a family has with service providers is part of an informal, continuing opportunity for that family to identify the concerns, priorities, and resources that it brings to early intervention and the IFSP process. Bailey (in press) described this opportunity:

Principles for Identifying Family Concerns, Priorities, and Resources

- The inclusion of family information in the IFSP is voluntary on the part of families.
- The identification of family concerns, priorities, and resources is based on an individual family's determination of which aspects of family life are relevant to the child's development.
- A family need or concern exists only if the family perceives that the need or concern exists.
- Families have a broad array of formal and informal options to choose from in determining how they will identify their concerns, priorities, and resources.
- Families have multiple and continuing opportunities to identify their concerns, priorities, and resources.
- Family confidences are respected, and family-shared information is not discussed casually among staff.
- The process of identifying family concerns, priorities, and resources leads to the development of IFSP outcomes, strategies, and activities that help families achieve the things they want from early intervention for their children and themselves.

Phone calls, home visits, clinic appointments, medical rounds, arrival and departure times, and diagnostic sessions all provide opportunities for obtaining information about family needs, perceptions, and resources.

Such an informal approach to identifying family concerns, priorities, and resources is consistent with the findings of Summers and her colleagues (1990). In a series of focus groups, families consistently stressed the importance of informal, open-ended approaches to this aspect of the IFSP process. Bailey (in press), however, emphasized that considerable variability exists in family preferences for how these activities are conducted, and recommended that an individual's preference be determined and the approach tailored to that preference.

A family's agenda changes over time as family circumstances, concerns, resources, priorities, and choices change. Multiple and continuing opportunities to identify concerns and priorities also limit the intrusiveness of gathering information from families. Families feel free to choose how much information to share or reveal at any given time when they know they will have many other chances to share things in the future (McGonigel & Garland, 1988). Early intervention programs and professionals should look at all interactions with a family as opportunities for the family to share with staff any updates, revisions, or other changes of family priorities and choices.

The Parents as Partners Project (1988) at Alta Mira in Albuquerque, New Mexico, advised parents in the program on how they can direct the process of identifying family concerns, priorities, and resources:

> You may choose what information you want to share. . . . You should never feel that you have to share any information about your family that you do not feel comfortable sharing. (p. 2)

- **Family confidences are respected, and family-shared information is not discussed casually among staff.**

Most early intervention practitioners are well accustomed to ensuring that information and records about individual children and families are kept confidential. Access is afforded to other professionals outside the program or agency only with the written consent of a child's parent or legal guardian.

Professionals are often less careful, however, about sharing family information with colleagues in casual settings, such as the lunchroom or hallway.

Many families can give examples of overhearing conversations about themselves or about other families that left them feeling embarrassed and angry over the violation of their privacy. Careful attention to what family information can be shared with other team members and to where such discussions occur are necessary to true confidentiality of family information.

- **The process of identifying family concerns, resources, and priorities leads to the development of IFSP outcomes, strategies, and activities that help families achieve the things they want from early intervention for their children and themselves.**

Asking someone to share information about his or her needs and concerns implies a promise to help (Black, Prestridge, & Anderson, 1981). This promise is kept only when the needs and concerns that families share as part of the IFSP process are translated into outcomes and formal and informal resources are mobilized to meet those outcomes.

Methods and Measures

There are a variety of informal and formal methods and measures currently being used to help families identify their concerns, priorities, and resources as part of the IFSP process. Some approaches are consistent with the family-centered principles described in Chapter Two; some clearly are not. Any method or measure in this process should be carefully screened by consulting family members to ensure that it is respectful of families -- non-intrusive, non-judgmental, and (if written) written in plain, jargon-free language (Woodruff, et al., 1990).

Interviews, Conversations, and Chats

Families come to early intervention programs and services with concerns about their children. If, during these first contacts, professionals truly listen to families, an atmosphere of honesty and mutuality develops. Summers and colleagues (1990) reported the importance families in their focus groups placed on "the willingness of professionals to invest time in developing rapport" with families (p. 87).

Interviews, conversations, chats, storytelling, brainstorming -- there are a variety of strategies for identifying family concerns, priorities, and resources that are based on listening to and talking with families. Recognizing the importance of face-to-face discussions between families and staff, Winton and Bailey (1990) emphasized the need for early intervention professionals to develop their family interviewing and communication skills within the context of their particular work environments. Interviews with families as part of the IFSP process can be formal or informal, structured or unstructured, depending on family choice and professional ability.

In addition to interviews and other traditional strategies for gathering information about family concerns, priorities, and resources, there are a variety of creative approaches available to staff and families. Brainstorming is one such approach. Brainstorming can help families recognize the many resources and talents they have that can be used to benefit their infant or toddler with special needs. Such informal exchanges are often more helpful in identifying family concerns and resources than the use of formal measures. As families talk about the things they like to do, this information can form the basis for later IFSP activities.

One family's love of music, for example, may provide opportunities for language development or social interaction. Another family's organizational skills may greatly assist in maintaining accurate records of services and developmental changes. A particular family's attitudes, beliefs, and coping style are other factors that family members may identify as strengths and resources to be used in developing and implementing the IFSP.

Another creative approach, "talk story," is common in many Hawaiian communities. Staff and families gather and exchange information relevant to early intervention by interweaving such information into the ordinary ebb and flow of everyday conversation, without explicit reference to the exchange (Roberts, 1990).

All of the listening/talking approaches to identifying family concerns, priorities, and resources require that professionals have finely tuned listening skills. Turnbull and her colleagues (1991) identified several "pointers for listening" that can be used to guide professionals through this aspect of the IFSP process:

a. Listen for cultural and family values that are important to the family.

b. Listen for the names of family members, friends, and professionals who are already in the support network and whose support has been particularly valued.

c. Listen for interests, needs, strengths that might link the child and family with a wider network of supporters.

d. Listen for the coping strategies that the family uses and any expressed desire for expanding coping strategies.

e. Listen for things that the family would like to do to help their child and to help themselves (to-do list).

f. Listen for how the family has typically approached solving problems in the past.

g. Listen for concerns, hopes, and plans that the families have concerning transitional issues.

h. Listen for the kinds of evaluations that have been conducted in the past and the evaluation questions that they would like to have addressed.

i. Listen for and acknowledge the specific strengths the family has shown in adjusting to their child's disability in meeting the child's needs. (p. 2)

Written Measures

Checklists, inventories, surveys, and questionnaires can help a family identify its concerns and resources relative to family priorities. Such written measures can be either formal or informal, depending on how they are structured and how they are used.

Many written instruments developed for this purpose are self-assessment measures that family members can use to check off areas and activities that they feel represent their concerns and priorities. There are many different ways in which such measures can be used by staff and families. Some families prefer to use self-assessment measures privately, sharing with program staff at a later time only that information they find relevant to their family agendas. Other families prefer that a staff member use a family self-assessment measure as a guide for a face-to-face interview. The very best way to discover how family members would like to identify their concerns, priorities, and resources is to *ask* them.

It may help families to think about the resources they have available to them to meet family concerns when such potential resources are organized in a series of general categories, such as financial resources, physical resources, social support, physical and emotional health, and so on. Table 9 on page 62 lists major sources of support that can become resources for meeting family needs.

The following measures, which are included in Appendix D, can help a family identify its concerns, priorities, and resources:

- *Family Needs Survey, Revised Edition* (Bailey & Simeonsson, 1990b)
- *How Can We Help?* (Child Development Resources, 1988)
- *Parent Needs Survey* (Darling, 1988)
- *Family Needs Scale* (Dunst, Cooper, Weeldreyer, Synder, & Chase, 1988)
- *Family Support Scale* (Dunst, Jenkins, & Trivette, 1984)
- *Exercise: Social Support* (Summers, Turnbull, & Brotherson, 1985)

All of the above measures are designed to help families identify their concerns, priorities, resources, and sources of support specifically related to early intervention and other services. They are *not* "family assessment" instruments.

Writing for the IFSP Task Force work group concerned with this issue, Ann Turnbull described such inappropriate measures:

> There are a host of psychosocial instruments that measure stress, depression, locus of control, and numerous other personality characteristics and life circumstances. Such measures are not recommended for the purpose of identifying family strengths and needs as part of the IFSP process. The need to limit identification of family strengths and needs to those areas that a family decides are relevant to its family agenda places these standardized family assessment instruments out of context for the purposes of developing most IFSPs.
>
> If, however, a family does ask for help with family or marital relationships, individual counseling, or similar areas, then one or more of these measures may be appropriate for use with that particular family or individual family member. Staff who administer such instruments or counsel families in these areas should be specifically trained to do so. (Johnson, McGonigel, & Kaufmann, 1989, p. 38)

As early intervention professionals consider how they will help families identify their concerns, priorities, and resources, it is important to ensure that there is a match between the areas addressed by any measure chosen and the priority areas that a family identifies. For example:

> The Christopher family (described in Chapter Three, on pages 18-19) had no clear idea of what services they would like from the early intervention program for their child and themselves. The Christophers told their IFSP team that, as new parents of a baby with Down syndrome, they hadn't had much of a chance to think about what they wanted for Winnie. They wanted to know what kinds of services might be available and asked their team about other parents in similar circumstances.
>
> Because the Christophers were not sure about what they needed or wanted from the program, their service coordinator helped them think about possible areas of need by asking them if they would like to complete the *Family Needs Survey* (Bailey & Simeonsson, 1990b). The survey helped the Christophers think about the help they might like from the program in a variety of areas including information, support, explaining to others, community services, finances, and family functioning. The Christophers chose to take the survey home to think about and talk over with each other.
>
> As they filled out the survey together, the Christophers realized that the early intervention program could help them find other services for Winnie and could also help them talk to Winnie's grandparents, both sets of whom were asking many questions that the Christophers weren't sure how to answer. The *Family Needs Survey* was just one of the ways in which their IFSP team helped the Christophers think about their concerns and resources as the parents of a newly diagnosed infant.

The Christophers' service coordinator chose a measure that helped them think about their needs in several broad categories. This choice was a good match for the Christophers because they were not sure about their immediate priorities for early intervention services. Some families, however, come to an early intervention program with a clear and well-defined idea about what they want for their children and themselves. For such a family, asking them to complete a comprehensive survey of their strengths or needs may not be helpful -- in fact, it may be intrusive. For example:

> The DeLeon family (also described in Chapter Three, on page 18) referred themselves to an early intervention program on the recommendation of a member of their hospital medical team. The DeLeons' son, Manuel,

needed periodic monitoring of his development. They met with someone from the early intervention program and shared Manuel's hospital assessment records and their current priorities.

As a result of this discussion, the DeLeons and their IFSP team were able to develop the initial IFSP at their first meeting with the program. No additional assessment information about Manuel was necessary, and the DeLeons were clear that they did not want other services from the program at that time. The IFSP team helped the DeLeons think about their strengths and needs relative to getting Manuel's development monitored. They talked about whether or not the DeLeons had transportation to the center and the best times for the monitoring visits.

For this family, a discussion with the other members of their IFSP team was the best way to identify family concerns and resources relative to its priorities for its child and itself.

As professionals consider how best to help an individual family identify its concerns, priorities, and resources in a manner that is not intrusive, it is important that assumptions not be made about a family's sense of what is possible in their relationship with an early intervention program. One mother of twins with special needs shared her experiences:

> When the twins were babies, we had a lot of interaction with many different professionals. We talked with our service coordinator about our family's strengths and needs and about the areas that we needed help with -- things like equipment, home nursing help, early intervention home visits, and various therapies. I guess we seemed like we knew just what we wanted. No one ever told us that we *could* share our need for financial assistance, so we never said anything about it. It was six months later that we discovered we had been eligible for some assistance all along.

A Family Strengths Paradigm

Central to any family-centered approach to the identification of family concerns, priorities, and resources is the presumption of family strength and competence (Davis & Kaufmann, 1990; McGonigel, 1990; Trivette, Dunst, et al., 1990). Such an enabling approach builds on the strength present in all families and creates opportunities for a family to acquire new competencies to meet the outcomes it chooses for its child and itself (Dunst, Trivette, et al., 1988).

Many professionals, however, are more adept at identifying or helping families identify needs and concerns than strengths and resources. The IFSP process allows professionals to develop new skills in recognizing family strengths and resources. To take advantage of this opportunity, many professionals may need to reorient themselves. Don Edwards, Executive Director of PANOS, an international development organization, described such a reorientation on his journey toward family-centered care:

> [I]t became clear to me that I had to relearn many things about my notions of pathology and my notions of how families bond. I had to overcome some of my own middle class assumptions about my own people -- people who I somehow felt I was supposed to represent and empower, but in fact, knew very little about.
>
> One of the first things that becomes important for us to realize in dealing with these children and families is that they are successful families. They are not pathological families, as much of our training has led us to believe. They are families who, in their own ways, are doing the best they can with the least that they have. They are families who, despite the multigenerations that live in the home, have articulated a clear system of activity and decision making that is bound, in some ways, by many age-old traditions.
>
> Whether [families] are newly arrived immigrants, or have been in this country since slavery times like my people, we must recog-

nize that they bring an expectation and a willingness, and, in fact, a practice of solving their problems and running their lives in such a way that they will achieve certain goals. (Edwards, 1989)

Cultural Competence

Implicit in recognizing family strengths and competence is knowledge that:

> all cultures are intrinsically healthy . . . any given culture existing within its own world of experience has developed those behavioral standards, values, symbols, and mythic framework which enable it to successfully sustain itself. One definition of racism is the habit of placing one's own cultural values onto the people of other cultures. (Jones, 1985, p. 4)

Culturally competent professionals understand the power of culture in shaping both family and professional beliefs, attitudes, and practices. Hanson and her colleagues (1990) identified four tasks that will help early intervention practitioners become more culturally competent:

> First, they must clarify their own values and assumptions. Second, they must gather and analyze ethnographic information regarding the cultural community within which each family resides. Third, they must determine the degree to which the family operates transculturally; and, finally, they must examine each family's orientation to specific child-rearing issues. (p. 126)

Honoring family diversity creates a solid foundation for the family/professional partnerships that are essential to the success of the IFSP process.

Supporting Family Strength

Professionals empower families by recognizing and supporting existing family strengths and resources. Lisbeth Vincent (1988) described how professionals can be most supportive of families:

> Families are succeeding because they are able to build support networks which they can call upon when their individual resources are not enough to solve their problems. Parents are most likely to rely upon family members, friends, neighbors, or coworkers for support when confronting problems in raising their children. Only as a last resort do they consult professionals. . . . we need to focus more of our attention on helping families develop and strengthen their own support networks. We need to emphasize to families that they are the ones best able to solve their own problems. (p. 3)

Respecting families for who they are and for the creative responses they have made to life enables professionals to ask "What resources and supports are present in your family? How can we build, together, on this foundation?" (D. A. Jones, personal communication, February 1991). As families and professionals work together over time, the shared joys of success and disappointments of failure provide a rich arena for the continuing identification of family concerns, priorities, and resources.

Developing the IFSP: Outcomes, Strategies, Activities, and Services

By Shirley Kramer, Mary J. McGonigel, and Roxane K. Kaufmann

Introduction

This chapter recommends approaches to developing family-centered IFSP outcomes and to identifying the strategies, activities, and services that will help bring about these outcomes. During this phase of the IFSP process, the IFSP team has an opportunity to review all of the information they have gathered and exchanged, to prioritize family choices, and to negotiate how these choices can best be honored.

The concept of "outcomes" may still be new to many professionals. Most teachers and therapists have had years of practice writing "goals and objectives" for children as part of the Individualized Educational Program (IEP) process required by Public Law 94-142, a process that, in practice, is primarily professionally directed. These goals and objectives are usually behavioral and tend to focus on professionally prescribed strategies and activities designed to bring about child change. Many early intervention professionals have been accustomed to a very similar approach in their work with infants and toddlers. With the implementation of the IFSP component of Part H, however, many professionals are learning about the differences between IEP goals and objectives and IFSP outcomes.

Definitions and Descriptors

To clarify these differences, it may be helpful to define terms. IEP *goals and objectives* are the short- and long-term behaviors that are the targets of special education or therapeutic intervention. IEP objectives are almost always behavioral -- specifying the target behavior in operational terms, describing under what conditions the behavior will be demonstrated, and listing both the criteria that will be used to evaluate achievement of the objective and the projected timelines for achievement.

The Expert Team and Task Force defined an IFSP *outcome* as a statement of the changes family members want to see for their child or themselves. An outcome can focus on any area of child development or family life that a family feels is related to its ability to enhance the child's development. An outcome must be functionally stated in terms of what is to occur (process) and what is expected as a result of these actions (product) (Dunst, Trivette, et al., 1988).

For example:

> **Vignette #3** -- Eating and talking were areas for Jennifer that Olivia Lain and the other members of the IFSP team wanted to work on. The outcome related to this need is as follows: Jennifer will increase her oral motor skills in order for her to eat more easily and to be able to make more sounds.

This outcome, specifically addressing Jennifer's oral motor skills, is very similar to an IEP long-term goal, and the strategies and activities that accompany the outcome were written almost exactly as they would have been for an IEP. Some programs are choosing to write child-related outcomes with accompanying behavioral objectives.

Other programs are exploring with families ways to develop outcomes that deliberately depart from this IEP style.

For example:

> **Vignette #1** -- Mealtimes were difficult times for Theresa and her daughter Julie because Mary ate poorly and was very fussy. The outcome related to this concern is as follows: Theresa and Julie want some help with mealtimes so that Mary can learn how to eat more foods, be less fussy, and grow stronger.

This outcome, like the one in the previous example, reflects family concerns about eating, but it addresses the issue within the larger context of mealtimes. The strategies and activities chosen to address Theresa's and Julie's concern were described in everyday language, very differently from the language commonly used for IEP objectives.

It is in the area of outcomes that primarily concern the family that the distinction between IEP behavioral objectives and IFSP outcomes becomes most significant. Many early intervention professionals are convinced that the concept of writing behavioral objectives for adult family members is inconsistent with an enabling and empowering approach to families. McGonigel and Garland (1988) illustrated this concern by providing an example of an inappropriate "family" outcome developed by staff in one program:

> When the home visitor arrives at the home, Mrs. Smith will be up and dressed and will have Travis dressed and fed at least 90% of the time. (p.19)

Although this outcome meets the criteria for an acceptable behavioral objective, it obviously does not meet criteria for family-centered services such as being respectful, enabling, and based on family-identified need.

Family Language

Just as it is important to use the family's language during the assessment, it is equally important to use the family's language in wording outcomes. A family will be more likely to feel ownership of the IFSP if the written document contains the same kind of language family members used when discussing their priorities.

> **Family Language:** We want some help with teaching our other children why their little sister is slow, and about how they can explain it to their friends at school.
>
> **Professional Jargon:** The siblings will attend a sibling support group in order to gain a developmentally appropriate understanding of Down syndrome.

For example, a family may say "We want some help with teaching our other children about why their little sister is slow, and about how they can explain it to their friends at school." If, in the process of writing down this family-desired outcome, a professional member of the team writes "the siblings will attend a sibling support group in order to gain a developmentally appropriate understanding of Down syndrome," the family may lose all sense of that outcome as theirs. Outcomes written in professional language also increase the likelihood that professionals will forget that the IFSP belongs, first and foremost, to the family.

Collaborative Development of the IFSP

Selecting IFSP outcomes, strategies, activities, and services should be done in a way that reflects the same family-centered, collaborative philosophy that characterizes the other aspects of the IFSP process. It is at this point in the development of the IFSP that differences and conflicts most often surface between families and staff.

The potential for such conflict is inherent in the differences that commonly exist between the values, perspectives, and priorities of professionals and families. Early intervention professionals often think of themselves as advocates for the infants and toddlers with special needs with whom they work. By training and, frequently, by inclination, many professionals focus solely on maximizing the development of the child who is their patient, client, or student. Unfortunately, maximizing developmental opportunities for the child with special needs is sometimes done at the expense of other members of the family or of the family as a whole.

A family is more likely, however, to view its child with special needs in the context of the entire family. The family is concerned with balancing the needs of this one child with the needs of other family members and the family as a unit. This difference in emphasis is just one of the many differences in the ways that families and professionals view the world.

Given the inherent difference in perspective that is reflected in the differing values and priorities of families and professionals, negotiation, collaboration, and mutual problem solving must be the foundation of a family-centered team process for developing the IFSP.

New Skills for Professionals and Families

A truly collaborative team process for selecting IFSP outcomes, strategies, activities, and services may require that both families and professionals learn new skills. Bailey (1987) listed five basic skills professionals need to work collaboratively with families. Among these skills are the ability to (1) look at families from a systems perspective; (2) identify relevant family needs; (3) use appropriate listening and interviewing techniques; (4) negotiate with families to reach joint solutions; and (5) help families match their needs with available resources in their community.

Parents and other family members involved in this collaborative team process also need certain skills. Among these are the ability to (1) determine their priorities from among multiple needs and desires; (2) communicate their strengths and needs clearly; (3) share information about their child; (4) listen to and evaluate assessment information; (5) weigh service options to determine which most closely meet their needs and match their preferences; (6) ask for clarification, additional information, or help in making difficult decisions or choices; and (7) work with service providers to ensure that services are delivered in a way that is supportive rather than disruptive of family values and family life. Table 8 is a checklist developed by families for families to help them examine how they are doing

Table 8
Partnership Checklist

- Am I honest with team members about my child's abilities and skill level?
- Do I share information about my child and family that will help determine the services we need?
- Am I committed to the plan as outlined . . . that is, will I take responsibility for some of the strategies?
- Am I contributing to the plan in any way? (Equipment, ideas, time, decisions?)
- When I disagree or am disappointed, do I talk to the team about it, instead of to other people who are not involved?
- Do I ask for clarification, additional information, or help in making difficult decisions or choices?
- Am I effective in persuading team members of the importance of my family's priorities and values -- can I negotiate some compromises without demanding?
- Do I respect the knowledge, skill and experience of other team members, and also respect their time, schedules, and priorities?

Source: Hunt, M., Cornelius, P., Leventhal, P., et al. (1990). *Into our lives*. Akron, OH: Children's Hospital Medical Center.

in using such team skills to build partnerships with professionals.

Family Direction

Ideally, the result of a collaborative team process will be mutually acceptable outcomes and corresponding strategies, activities, and services. In those instances in which the staff and the family are not able to agree on service priorities, however, the IFSP outcomes should reflect the priorities and values of the family rather than the staff. As Bailey (1987) noted:

> Interventionists may need to sacrifice strong beliefs about intervention . . . in favor of collaborative goal-setting. If parents do not agree with or are not interested in interventionist priorities for treatment, those treatments are doomed to failure. (p.69)

This principle of family direction does not mean that professionals abdicate their responsibility for communicating their perspectives on desired outcomes for the infant or toddler with special needs. Indeed, honest and open communication with a family about these professional perspectives is a cornerstone of the collaborative IFSP process. Such communication enables the family to make informed decisions after considering the viewpoints presented by the professionals. When the staff and the family do not agree on choices for IFSP outcomes, however, the family's choices ultimately take precedence.

A frequently expressed concern about family direction in early intervention is that *all* families of children with special needs will not *always* make the best choices for *every* child. While this is undoubtedly true, it is equally true of families whose children have no special needs. Parents of children with special needs have the same right to family autonomy as do other parents.

The exceptions that apply to family decision making in early intervention are the same child protection considerations that apply for all children. In situations that can be considered abuse or neglect, professional responsibility is clear and usually prescribed in state law. In situations that fall short of child abuse or neglect, yet involve parent actions that are clearly detrimental to the child, professionals should convey their concerns in an open, honest, and direct fashion. Such communication is more likely to be successful if the professionals have initially developed positive, collaborative relationships with the family (Bailey, 1987).

Negotiation

Family values are not negotiable. What is negotiable, however, are the strategies, activities, and services that the entire team will use to help bring about the family's chosen outcomes. Negotiation between families and professionals during this process can include the following elements:

- information sharing;
- active listening;
- perception checking;
- compromise;
- formal agreements to reconsider or reintroduce at another time; and
- decisions to ask other people to join the team to clarify information or to gain insight.

As these elements demonstrate, the purpose of negotiation is not to give professionals a forum to convince families that professional points of view should prevail. Rather, negotiation creates an environment in which staff and family members can discuss competing priorities, investigate alternatives and options, and choose the strategies, activities, and services that will bring about the family's desired outcomes.

Although family choices should always prevail in the selection of IFSP outcomes, it is not always possible for family choices to be met in the selection of strategies, activities, and services. Available services will depend, to some extent, on how the state system of early intervention interprets its legal obligation under Part H. Other considerations include limited staff time and resources and the potential negative consequences of service choices.

Some families, for example, may request strategies, activities, or services to meet their desired outcomes that are beyond the ability of the early intervention system to provide:

> Shana Anderson is a two year old who lives in a small town in Montana. She was diagnosed last year with mild cerebral palsy and has been receiving physical therapy at home once a week. The early intervention program staff would like to have a child development specialist also visit Shana and Mrs. Anderson once a week to work on Shana's other developmental needs. Mrs. Anderson, however, wants to return to work and have Shana attend a child care center.
>
> In a recent IFSP team meeting, Mrs. Anderson asked the early intervention program to find and pay for a good child care program for Shana. Since Shana's developmental needs do not require daily developmental intervention, the early intervention program could not pay for child care for Shana. The service coordinator agreed to help Mrs. Anderson locate a good child care program and to investigate ways that Mrs. Anderson could get some help to pay for it.
>
> Because Mrs. Anderson wanted to go back to work, the team also decided that home visits were not a good way to deliver services. The team agreed that Shana would receive her physical therapy at the child care center and that the child development specialist would consult with the staff at the center to help them plan appropriate activities.

Some families will request strategies, activities, or services that are within the responsibility of the early intervention system to provide, but that are of a frequency or intensity that is beyond the limits of available resources. When a family requests needed services that an early intervention program can neither provide nor help to arrange, the IFSP can serve as a powerful tool for advocacy. Families and professionals can use the IFSP to demonstrate unmet needs of children and families to local and state Interagency Coordinating Councils. Service coordinators are responsible for advocating for needed services when there are gaps in the local service delivery system. They also are responsible for helping those families who wish to be self-advocates acquire the necessary skills to do so.

Some families may choose strategies, activities, or services that are unlikely to result in their desired outcomes being met. In such instances, the professional members of the team are responsible for sharing their knowledge and experience with the family in such a way that the family can evaluate alternatives and options. For example:

> Crystal Jones expressed her desire to do "everything possible" for her infant son, Tommy, who was born blind. In discussions with her IFSP team, Crystal decided on more and more outcomes she wanted to work toward. She wanted the early intervention program to address each of Tommy's developmental needs or potential needs. Crystal also wanted to learn as much as she could about the effect of Tommy's blindness on his development. She thought she should go back to school to take special education and therapy courses, but she worried that she didn't have the time or energy.
>
> The other members of the team were concerned that Crystal was trying to take on too much and to work on too many outcomes at the same time. They helped Crystal prioritize her many desired outcomes, decide where to start, and limit the number of projects she and the rest of the team would undertake at one time. For example, Crystal decided that the home visitor could help her gain knowledge and skills through a "parent as therapist" curriculum and that taking courses was an activity that she could consider for the future.

Building on Family Strengths and Resources

After identifying a possible outcome, the team considers the strengths and resources of the child, family, program, and community that can contribute to the child's and family's ability to achieve the outcome. All of the information gathered and shared between staff and families up to this point in the IFSP process is reviewed. A systematic consideration of specific child and family strengths and resources for addressing child needs and family choices forms the basis for selecting the strategies and activities that support outcome implementation.

Some families will need little help examining the resources and support available to help them meet their chosen outcomes. Such families may have a clear idea of who they want to help implement specific outcomes and activities, of the insurance or other financial resources that are available to them, and of any other support that they may need to meet their desired IFSP outcomes. For example:

Manuel DeLeon's development had been monitored by his parents and staff from the local early intervention program ever since he was released from the hospital. When Manuel was two and a half years old, the occupational therapist in the program became concerned about the quality of his motor patterns. The IFSP team met to discuss possible changes in Manuel's outcomes and decided that he would receive occupational therapy once a week and that the therapist would work with the staff at his child care center to teach them ways to increase the variety and quality of Manuel's motor patterns.

As soon as these changes were suggested, the DeLeons were able to figure out how they wanted to manage things. Mr. DeLeon's mother would be able to drive Manuel to therapy, their private insurance would pay for it, and the child care center staff had offered many times in the past to work with anyone they needed to help Manuel, who was a favorite at the center.

Other families may not have had the opportunity to consider possible sources of formal and informal support that they could use to achieve the outcomes they desire for their children and themselves. Often families short-change themselves by failing to recognize their own resources that can be valuable contributions to bringing about their desired outcomes. For such families, it may be necessary to explore a number of options and possibilities in a structured way.

For example:

Vignette #4 -- When the Mack family met with Project LIFT to develop Lita's first IFSP, they were not sure whether they had anyone who could be helpful to them in implementing the outcomes they wanted for Lita. As the parents of a very fragile child, Dee and Mark were feeling alone.

Table 9
Major Sources of Support for Meeting Family Needs

Support Sources	Members
Nuclear Family	Spouse, mate, children, other household members
Kinship	Blood and marriage relatives
Informal Network	Friends, neighbors, church associates, co-workers, etc.
Social Organizations	Church, service clubs, parent-to-parent support groups, etc.
Professionals	Pediatricians and other medical specialists, day care providers, hospital and school personnel, early intervention program staff, speech therapists, occupational and physical therapists, etc.
Policy Makers	Agency directors, school boards, city councils, state representatives, etc.

Source: Dunst, C. J., Trivette, C. M., & Deal, A. G. (1988). *Enabling and empowering families: Principles and guidelines for practice.* Cambridge, MA: Brookline.

Their IFSP team used a technique called an "Eco Map" to help the Macks think about people in their life who might become resources for meeting Lita's IFSP outcomes. As the Macks talked with staff about the people who were important in their lives, LIFT staff turned this information into a map. Dee and Mark were able to see that there were many professionals, neighbors, and friends who were possible sources of support in bringing about the IFSP outcomes they had chosen. The Eco Map helped the team develop specific activities and strategies for each outcome.

Figure 2 on the following page shows the Macks' completed Eco Map as an example of one approach to identifying possible sources of support.

Encouraging a family to employ its own support network strengthens families and reduces the possibility that the family will become overly dependent on the service system (Trivette, Deal, & Dunst, 1986). At the Family, Infant and Preschool Program in North Carolina, families work with staff to develop creative ways to use their own resources to meet family needs. For example, one family in the program had a car, but had no money at all in their budget to buy gasoline. Another family had no car, but they did have enough money to buy some gasoline. Both families needed occasional transportation. These two families were linked by their service coordinators. Now, they routinely trade their resources with each other to meet a joint need, relying on each other rather than on professionals.

Building on family strengths and resources before making use of professional resources is a basic principle for enabling and empowering families in early intervention.

Strategies and Activities

The strategies, activities, and services that will be used to bring about a family's chosen outcomes grow naturally out of the process of identifying and reviewing child, family, program, and community strengths and resources available to meet outcomes. Family and professional actions needed to bring about IFSP outcomes should be clearly stated as part of the strategies, activities, and services included in the plan.

For example:

Vignette #3 -- As Jennifer made more developmental progress, Barbara (her mother) felt more comfortable playing with her and thought perhaps she would like to become a part of Jenny's early intervention program. Olivia (Jenny's guardian) decided she would like Barbara to be able to participate. The outcome developed for this need was: Jennifer's home program will be adapted in order to involve Barbara to the level and extent she desires.

The following are the activities and strategies to achieve this outcome: (1) The service coordinator will request a meeting with Barbara to discuss her interest in participation in early intervention activities; (2) The team will make adaptations in the plan as determined by Barbara, with Olivia's consent and approval; (3) The service coordinator will meet with Barbara, as negotiated; (4) The service coordinator will offer home visits in a neutral setting (e.g. church, community center).

The IFSP team member who is responsible is stated for each activity, so that every person involved knows what he or she is to do to bring about a particular outcome. Family members who agree to perform specific tasks should be involved in the planning and decision-making process to the maximum extent desired by and appropriate for each family member.

For example:

Vignette #1 -- Julie Crowder is an important source of help and support to her mother and little sister, Mary. Because of her interest in helping out with Mary's care, Julie was involved in the IFSP process from the start. She went with her mother and the social worker to the first meeting at the early intervention program, and she was able to talk about her concerns with the rest of the IFSP team. As a result of this early involvement, Julie was able to get some support for her needs at the same time she was volunteering to be responsible for picking Mary up at child care and for working with the homemaker who would be visiting the Crowders' home to help with mealtimes.

The degree to which IFSP outcomes can be met depends on many factors, including the extent to which the following conditions are met:

Figure 2

Eco Map

Child's Name: Lita
Date: May 28, 1989

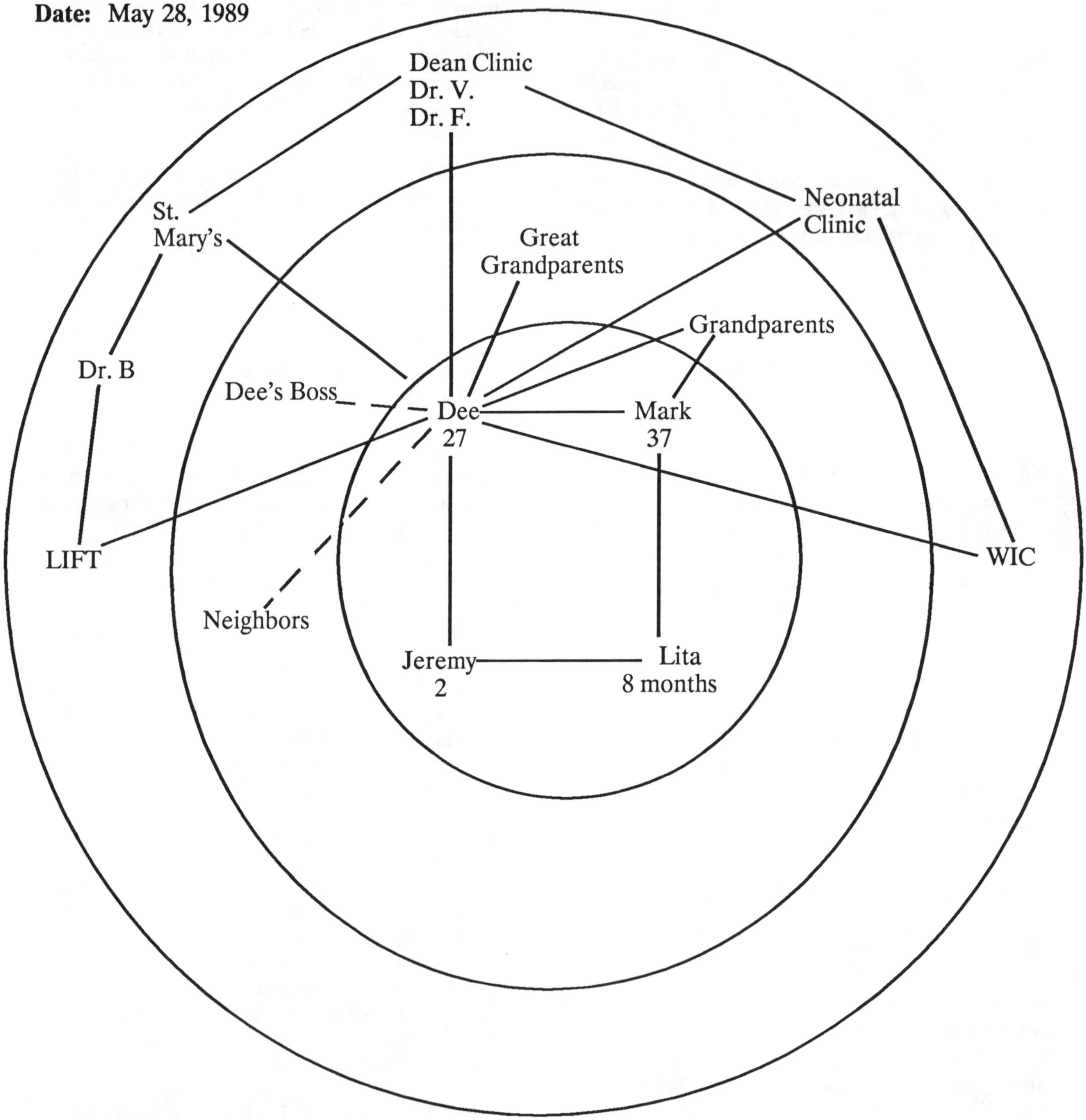

——— close ties or possible support
– – – not close or friction

- the outcome is functionally stated;
- the outcome represents a family's priorities and choices;
- strategies and activities are practical and fit with a family's ordinary schedule; and
- strategies or activities focus on mobilizing a family's own resources and support network (Dunst, Trivette, et al., 1988).

The Parents as Partners Project (1988) illustrated many of these issues in their IFSP guide for families:

> Carrying out [outcomes] should fit into your family's routines and job schedules. Anyone involved with your child can be included in working on the plan . . . Goals can be worked on in the home, grocery store, laundry mat, at Grandma's house, etc. . . . A trip to the grocery store could be turned into activities that support occupational therapy (sitting in the cart, handling the food) and speech therapy (learning new words and sounds). (p.7)

Discovering strategies and activities that fit naturally into a family's daily life is a critical aspect of the IFSP process. Turnbull and Summers (1985) reflected on the demands professionals often place on parents' time at home, "anything is possible for those with no responsibility for implementation" (p.10).

Criteria and Timelines

Agreeing on criteria and timelines for evaluating the extent to which an outcome has been achieved is the final component of developing the IFSP. According to Bailey (1988), "[t]wo basic rules govern outcome specification. First, the measurement criteria should fit the intent of the [outcome]. . . . Second, there should be agreement as to whether the objective has been met" (p.240).

In other words, how will the team know when an outcome has been achieved? What will "success" look like to the family? When is it time to "quit" working toward an outcome? Just as the family's agenda is the main determinant of outcome selection, so should the family's definition of success be the primary criteria for outcome evaluation. Table 10 provides a rating scale that one program uses for evaluating outcome achievement.

Format and Forms

The Individualized Family Service Plan, if it is to be successful, must be a fluid, living document. IFSP formats and forms should reflect this vitality. A form chosen for an IFSP is important because "it translates legislation and policy into procedures and actions" (Place, 1988, p. 10). An IFSP form can

Table 10
Evaluation Rating Scale

Ratings	Criteria
1	Situation changed or worsened; no longer a need, goal, or project.
2	Situation unchanged; still a need, goal, or project.
3	Implementation begun; still a need, goal, or project.
4	Outcome partially attained or accomplished.
5	Outcome accomplished or attained; but not to the family's satisfaction.
6	Outcome mostly accomplished or attained to the family's satisfaction.
7	Outcome completely accomplished or attained to the family's satisfaction.

Source: Deal, A. G., Dunst, C. J., & Trivette, C. M. (1989). A flexible and functional approach to developing Individualized Family Support Plans. *Infants and Young Children*, *1*(4), 32-43.

provide an outline for the consensus-building team discussion that results in a family-centered IFSP.

Some states, such as Minnesota and Maryland, are choosing to develop one IFSP form that must be used by all Part H programs. Others, such as Texas and Virginia, are leaving the choice of forms to local programs. Whichever approach is taken, an IFSP form should promote rather than hinder a family-centered IFSP process.

The best format for the IFSP may be one that allows the IFSP team to record the process as it happens, rather than going back later to "fill in the form." To keep the IFSP dynamic and easily revised, some programs are choosing not to have IFSPs typed, but, instead, to write them by hand and leave them handwritten.

Because Part H requires that the IFSP contain a number of pieces of information not necessarily directly related to outcomes or activities (e.g., anticipated duration of services, transition provision, etc.), a cover sheet or a final sheet containing such information might be helpful.

Sample IFSPs

Sample Individualized Family Service Plans for the four families that have been followed in this monograph are provided in Appendix A. The Expert Team does not recommend or endorse any particular IFSP form or format. To illustrate the many creative possibilities, the IFSP developers were asked to use widely divergent formats, forms, and approaches. The Lains' IFSP, for example, includes an assessment summary and pertinent history. The Crowders' IFSP, on the other hand, includes only the child's developmental levels and a statement of the child's and family's strengths and needs. To ensure diversity in the sample plans, the IFSPs included in this document do not necessarily reflect the form or format used by the programs of which the IFSP developers are a part.

Similarly, the outcomes and activities that are included in these sample plans are not intended to represent the "answers" for these four children and families. Rather, the plans are presented to illustrate the principles and practices described in this monograph, as interpreted by four IFSP teams. In real situations, the actual document that is the IFSP cannot be evaluated without reference to the process that was used to develop and implement the plan. In the final analysis, only the families involved can determine if their IFSPs truly match the strengths, needs, resources, and aspirations of their children and themselves.

Implementation of the Individualized Family Service Plan

By Carl J. Dunst

Introduction

Implementation translates the written IFSP into action. Implementation refers to the processes, methods, and procedures used to attain IFSP outcomes. Implementation brings to life the plans to meet child and family needs. The ways in which implementation proceeds will largely determine whether or not children and families benefit from their IFSPs. Implementation should reflect beliefs about working with families that mirror a family-centered philosophy. If the IFSP is a "living document," then implementation is the lifeline that keeps the document alive.

This chapter outlines principles and conditions for implementation and provides guidelines for early intervention service coordination as part of IFSP implementation. Evaluation and protection of family rights are also discussed.

Implementation Principles

IFSP implementation is guided by the same family-centered philosophy that forms the foundation for all other components of the IFSP process. Several principles should guide implementation, so that plans are put into action in ways that support and strengthen family functioning. Informed decision making by families is the cornerstone of effective implementation. One decision will be the extent to which a family chooses to be involved in early intervention.

The following principles encourage active decision making and promote and strengthen family functioning:

- **Resources and services should reflect a range of options that are guided by the normalization principle.**

A full range of options ensures that families will have appropriate services and resources from which to choose; having a choice among services and resources promotes informed decision making by families. Providing those resources and services in the least restrictive and most integrative way possible helps the infant or toddler become or remain an integral member of the family and the family become or remain integral members of its neighborhood and community. Being part of a community "involves the coming together of people around shared values and the pursuit of a common cause" Hobbs, et al., 1984, p. 41).

- **Resources and services, to the extent possible, should be community based and provided in locations close to the family.**

Normalized services are those that are provided in a family's community or in locations where most families get needed resources. Community-based services help bring together people who share common beliefs and have common needs. Families who participate in community-based programs learn and benefit from each other. Part H regulations support this concept and caution against allowing early intervention services to isolate children and families from community life {303.12(b) and Note 1}.

- **Early intervention programs must be responsive to the broad-based needs of children and families, although no one program can be expected to provide all services to all families.**

Different families are likely to have quite different needs and concerns. This principle requires a highly responsive, individualized approach to the IFSP process. It does not require that one program or any one staff member be able to provide all necessary services and resources. Rather, facilitating linkages should be a major role of programs and staff members, helping to "identify family needs, locate the informal and formal resources necessary for meeting those needs, and . . . link families with the identified resources" (Hobbs et al., 1984, p. 50).

The interagency collaboration required by Part H is a critical aspect of meeting broad-based needs of children and families. Creative, collaborative interactions among agencies, families, and private practitioners can enable families and support their right to make choices. The experience of one family reflects this collaboration:

> A two-and-a-half year old boy with cerebral palsy and an accompanying seizure disorder was having difficulty processing auditory information. In addition to his physical disability, he also had significant speech and language delays. In frustration, he often either withdrew or acted out in temper tantrums. This behavior was causing his family a great deal of anxiety.
>
> After interviewing professionals recommended by the child's pediatrician and the early intervention team, the parents chose a specialist to help with the problem. She conducted assessments at home and in the community. Together, the specialist, parents, and early intervention staff developed strategies to address the behavior.
>
> The cost of the extra assessments by the specialist was billed to the family's private insurance provider; her consultation with the early intervention team was billed to the early intervention program; and the consultation time she spent with the parents and in-home respite providers was billed to the county that administers a waiver program under which the child is served. The result was a co-funded, comprehensive, meaningful, and effective intervention that met the child's needs and addressed the parents' concerns and anxieties.

- **Implementation of the IFSP should promote family independence and interdependence with members of the family's community.**

Independence refers to the capacity to identify needs, assess options for meeting those needs, and mobilize the resources required to support and strengthen family functioning. For a variety of reasons, a family may choose to be more or less independent at certain times. Their individual needs, cultural norms, family style, and choices should always be respected.

Interdependence refers to joint efforts between a family and members of its personal social network (extended family, friends, and community) that are designed to promote the well-being of all network members. One activity that has promoted interdependence for many families is family-to-family support and networking, both informal (parents attending the same center chatting together while they watch their children play) and formal (parent support groups and structured family-to-family activities through organizations such as Parents Reach Out or Parent-to-Parent).

Mimi, the mother of Ryan, a toddler participating in the Family Child Learning Center at the Children's Medical Center of Akron, described what one kind of parent-to-parent support has meant to her:

> Yes, we're the parents of children with handicaps . . . but we have talents and dreams and interests and goals in life, just like anyone else. The range of activities and programs encourages us to relate to each other as people, not simply in the context of what we're sharing through our child, although that's important.

Conditions for Implementation

Six conditions are essential for implementing the IFSP in ways that optimally influence family functioning and for ensuring that the IFSP is a responsive, individualized document.

1. Family/Professional Partnerships

To be most effective, IFSP implementation should occur within the context of family/professional collaboration and partnerships. Collaboration means working together toward a common goal, while partnership means the pooling of resources that can be used toward some joint interest. Dunst and Paget (in press) defined parent/professional partnerships as "an association between a family and one or more professionals who function collaboratively using agreed upon roles in pursuit of a common interest or goal."

Collaboration and partnerships develop from a recognition that joint efforts are more likely to result in achieving intended outcomes. Families and professionals have much to gain by pooling what they know in order to develop and implement the IFSP.

It may be helpful to compare family/professional partnerships with other kinds of more familiar partnerships. Dunst and Paget (in press) illustrated the best kind of partnership between families and professionals by describing the fiduciary aspect of business partnerships:

> all partners owe complete loyalty to the partnership, trust and honesty are expected at all times, no partner can engage in any activity which in any way conflicts with the partnership, and . . . each partner must fully disclose to one another any and all information that relates to the common interest or joint venture of the partnership.

It is hoped that professionals and families in early intervention will develop such open, two-way partnerships. Nevertheless, professionals and families may not have *equal* duties and responsibilities to their relationship, particularly in the beginning. As paid professionals in the exercise of their chosen profession, early intervention specialists must assume greater responsibility for ensuring the success of family/professional relationships. It is incumbent upon them to share all information openly and honestly right from the start and to treat families with respect and dignity. Families, however, may choose to withhold information, understanding, and support until such time as they feel a trusting relationship has been established. A true partnership can be said to exist only when both families and professionals are able to fully disclose all the "material" facts that affect their joint activity.

In their IFSP guidance book, *Into Our Lives*, Mimi Hunt and her co-authors (1990) asked other parents to think about the qualities they would look for in a business partner. Among the qualities parents identified as desirable in a business partner were: honesty, integrity, dedication, confidentiality, spirit of cooperation, ability to communicate clearly, respect, initiative, knowledge, interest, investment (commitment of time, money, skill, or labor), problem-solving ability, and negotiation skills.

Implementation Principles

- Resources and services should reflect a range of options that are guided by the normalization principle.
- Resources and services, to the extent possible, should be community based and provided in locations close to the family.
- Early intervention programs must be responsive to the broad-based needs of children and families, although no one program can be expected to provide all services to all families.
- IFSP implementation should promote family independence and interdependence with members of the family's community.

2. Responsiveness to Family Concerns

The processes used to develop and implement IFSPs must be sensitive to the fact that multiple influences affecting families cause the concerns and priorities of families and of individual family members to change over time. As desired outcomes change, implementation strategies and activities must respond to these changes.

For example:

Vignette #2 -- When the Griffins' IFSP was first written as part of Benjamin's discharge plan, Michael and Leslie felt that the plan met their family's needs by setting up the therapies that Ben needed from the hospital therapists. Three months later, however, the Griffins' desired outcomes changed. The stress of traveling long distances twice a week to the hospital for Ben's therapies was becoming too much for Leslie and was interfering with her ability to be a mother to her daughter, Caroline.

Although Ben's need for therapy did not change, the Griffins asked their pediatrician, who was their service coordinator, about changing the strategies and activities to meet that need. Dr. White and the Griffins worked with the physical therapist and the occupational therapist to develop a single set of therapy goals for Ben, combining strategies and activities for meeting his needs in both areas. Under the revised IFSP activities, Leslie takes Ben to the hospital only once a week, and the physical therapist and occupational therapist do a joint session, working together to give Ben the therapy he needs.

IFSP methods and procedures must be both flexible and functional, so that programs are continually responsive to the concerns, interests, and aspirations of families.

3. Building on Family Strengths

As Stoneman (1985) noted:

> Every family has strengths and, if the emphasis (of intervention) is on supporting strengths rather than rectifying weaknesses, chances of making a difference in the lives of children and their families is vastly increased. (p. 462)

Family strengths are competencies and capabilities that can be used to meet needs and obtain resources, such as flexibility, a sense of purpose, or a commitment to family life. Building on these strengths will make a family even stronger and more capable.

4. Implementation Strategies

The strategies that will be used to obtain needed resources should be devised and agreed upon by family members and the professional(s) who are working with them. Such strategies should be developed collaboratively, using partnerships as the means for developing courses of action. The courses of action should state what the family has agreed to do, as well as what others will do in order to achieve intended outcomes. Family members who volunteer or are asked to be part of carrying out the IFSP should have a role in the planning and decision-making process.

Any team member can ask for changes in the IFSP. All changes in the IFSP must be discussed with the family and agreed upon jointly before additions, deletions, or other changes are made.

5. Flexibility in Implementation

The IFSP document itself must be flexible and able to accommodate any changes that occur within a family. In contrast to the IEP, which typically has a predetermined review and revision schedule, the particular processes and mechanisms used to develop and revise the IFSP should be much more flexible and responsive to the changing concerns of families. The IFSP should be a working document that reflects as accurately as possible what is being done at any particular time in order to achieve stated outcomes.

6. Level of Family Involvement

The extent to which a family will be involved in the development and implementation of the IFSP must be determined by the family itself. Family members should decide both to what extent and how they wish to be involved in all aspects of the IFSP process.

Family involvement will likely change as family interests, needs, and circumstances change. For example, some families may choose to be very involved in early intervention and the IFSP when their children are very young, but may prefer to be less active when their children become toddlers and the mothers choose to go back to work. Conversely, for example, other families initially may feel unprepared to take on IFSP responsibilities and may choose to have professionals address their needs. As these families gain confidence, however, they may choose to take a more active role in the IFSP process. Later, these same families may choose once again to do less because of other family demands.

A family's role in early intervention should not be thought of as a linear progression toward more involvement with an early intervention program. Because many families have been made to feel guilty if they chose less involvement at a given time, families may need explicit support from staff if they make this choice.

The Parents as Partners Project (1988) at Alta Mira Specialized Family Services, Inc., advised other parents on this issue:

> You can set it up so that you have little involvement or total involvement in carrying out this plan. . . . Remember, you are part of your early intervention team. A member of the team can decide on what he or she can or cannot do and the rest of the team will understand. . . . Your Individualized Family Service Plan and anybody's level of involvement can be changed at any time. (p. 9)

Opportunities for Experimentation

Because the IFSP represents a shift in the way in which professionals typically have worked with families, programs should be given considerable latitude to experiment with the formats and processes they will use to develop and implement the IFSP. It is only through expanded opportunities that the strengths and weaknesses of different approaches to working with families can be determined. Any approach, however, should ensure that families are treated with respect and should be jointly evaluated by families and professionals. Several states and programs are evaluating their processes for developing and implementing IFSPs. West Virginia, for example, has developed evaluation forms for use by both families and staff involved in the state's pilot IFSP projects.

Service Coordination Principles

Although Part H uses the term "case management," many families and professionals have objected to the use of these words, which imply that children and families are "cases" to be "managed." Some commonly used replacements that seem more respectful are service coordinator, primary service provider, family resources coordinator, and care coordinator. Several states have substituted other terms for case management in their draft policies, and many professional and family organizations have recommended that the reauthorization of Part H use a term other than case management. Because "service coordination" is likely to replace "case management" in the upcoming reauthorization, service coordination and service coordinators are the terms used throughout this chapter.

The service coordination practices employed in developing and implementing the IFSP will largely determine whether or not the IFSP supports and strengthens the family. A number of principles should guide service coordination and IFSP implementation.

- **Service coordination models and practices should reflect the implicit and explicit intent of the IFSP.**

Service coordination as specified in Part H is intended to be an active process that promotes family capacities and competencies to obtain resources and services. Many existing service coordination models and practices are based on assumptions and presuppositions that make clients passive recipients of resources and services. Such models are clearly in direct opposition to the intent of the

Service Coordination Principles

- Service coordination models and practices should reflect the implicit and explicit intent of the IFSP.
- Service coordinators must be able to perform multiple roles in their work with families.
- The ability to act in a linkage capacity is perhaps the most important role of a service coordinator.
- Service coordinator roles and functions should support and strengthen family functioning.
- A single service coordinator should be responsible for helping a family gain access to needed resources.
- Families should have as much opportunity as possible to select a service coordinator as part of early intervention services.
- Service coordination practices should not create any additional burdens or strains on families.
- Service coordinators must be provided with the training necessary to learn the skills needed to work effectively with families and with professionals from other disciplines.
- Effective service coordination practices will reflect the family-centered philosophy and conceptual framework of the IFSP.

law. IFSP implementation should afford and create opportunities to develop and test enabling and empowering models of service coordination.

Service coordination should be family-centered rather than agency-centered. Agency-centered service coordination operates for the convenience of the service system and focuses on the efficiency of scheduling paper flow and cost containment. Family-centered service coordination in contrast, focuses on facilitating the achievement of families' outcomes in ways that reflect their values, beliefs, and chosen levels of involvement with early intervention.

Project Copernicus, an MCH SPRANS project at the Kennedy Institute in Baltimore, promotes family-centered service coordination. *Recognizing Family-Centered Care* (Edelman, 1991) is a training resource available from this project to help professionals examine the differences between system-centered, child-centered, and family-centered service coordination and the implications of those differences for children and families.

- **Service coordinators must be able to perform multiple roles in their work with families.**

In order to be responsive to the needs of children and families, case managers must be capable of engaging in numerous roles. These roles will depend on family concerns, priorities, outcomes, and courses of action to meet the outcomes in a family's Individualized Family Service Plan. Dunst, Trivette, et al. (1988) described these expanded roles as linking people, mobilizing family resources and support, facilitating the development of new support structures, moderating exchanges among the members of a family's formal and informal network, and consulting with families about issues or concerns. One important service coordination role is helping children and families obtain their rights and procedural safeguards as guaranteed in the Part H regulations {303.6(a)(1)}.

- **The ability to act in a linkage capacity is perhaps the most important role of a service coordinator.**

Service coordinators who perform this role help families become more knowledgeable about resources and service options, create opportunities for families to make informed decisions about the benefits and limitations of different options, link families with desired resources and services, and enhance family members' acquisition of competencies and their ability to function in similar roles if they so desire.

For example:

Vignette #1 -- Mrs. Crowder was able to work toward the outcomes she wanted for herself and her family when her primary service provider at the early intervention program linked her with other resources in the community, such as the local mental health organization that provided Mrs. Crowder with taxi vouchers she could use to attend her drug treatment program. When Mrs. Crowder discovered that the publicly funded child care program in her neighborhood had a long waiting list, her primary service provider linked her to a city agency that provided funds for Mary to go to a licensed home child care program down the street from the Crowders' apartment, where Mrs. Crowder could take Mary in the morning and Julie could pick her up on the way home from school in the afternoon.

- **Service coordinator roles and functions should support and strengthen family functioning.**

Any and all roles that service coordinators employ with families should support and strengthen a family and should avoid the development of family dependence on the service coordinator or on service delivery systems. Service coordinators should use strategies that enhance a family's ability to negotiate the support systems that offer needed resources. Enabling and empowering roles are preferred because they specifically aim to make a family more capable of identifying and meeting its needs.

- **A single service coordinator should be responsible for helping families gain access to needed resources.**

Many families participating in early intervention programs find themselves with two, three, or even more service coordinators. To the extent possible, a single service coordinator should be responsible for helping a family implement its IFSP. Procedures must be developed and put into practice that allow optimal coordination of services and resources to families.

Shirley Kramer, an IFSP Expert Team member and the mother of twin preschoolers with special needs, conveys the realities of coping with multiple service providers and the need for coordinated services:

> I put five colorful, plastic teddy bears representing the five members of my family, in the bottom of a large glass jar. Then, as I describe the many professionals who have interacted with my family since the boys' birth, I begin adding more teddy bears -- one bear for each professional -- until my family is buried beneath *156* professional teddy bears.

- **Families should have as much opportunity as possible to select a service coordinator as part of early intervention services.**

As difficult as this may seem, especially in rural areas where few or no options may be available, innovative mechanisms should be developed that allow families both to choose and to change service coordinators as their needs change. If service coordinators must be assigned to families, procedures must be developed that allow changes in service coordinators when families feel that their needs are not being adequately and respectfully addressed. As the following example illustrates, at the Family, Infant and Preschool Program (FIPP) in Morganton, North Carolina, a family is able to change its service coordinator when the need arises:

> When the Johnson family's service coordinator moved to another state, they were assigned a new service coordinator, Debbie. At first, everything seemed to go smoothly. Debbie was friendly, but rather traditional in her approach to services. Her work with the Johnsons focused on home-based, child level therapies for their daughter.
>
> About six months after Debbie became the Johnsons' service coordinator, Mrs. Johnson called the program coordinator to talk about her dissatisfaction with the services they were receiving. She explained that she and her husband had sincerely tried to work with Debbie, but that they felt their family needed help with some issues that Debbie was not addressing. Mrs. Johnson also described the problem as a personality conflict and asked about the possibility of changing service coordinators.

The program coordinator thanked Mrs. Johnson for calling, and they discussed possible options. The program coordinator suggested working with Debbie to correct the problem, with the understanding that if the situation did not improve to the Johnsons' satisfaction, a new service coordinator would be chosen. Mrs. Johnson replied that she and her husband had discussed things at length, and they preferred to have a new service coordinator right away.

Based on the Johnsons' wishes, Debbie was replaced as their service coordinator. The program coordinator also asked Mrs. Johnson if it was all right for her to share the specifics of their conversation with Debbie, in order to help her learn to improve her work with families. The program coordinator arranged to call the Johnsons in a month to see if they were happy with their new service coordinator.

As service coordinators in a rural program, staff at FIPP encounter the same difficulties with long distances between families, scheduling complexities, and full "caseloads" with which many early intervention programs deal. Nevertheless, the enabling and empowering approach at FIPP dictates that a family have control over the way in which the program becomes involved in its life.

- **Service coordination practices should not create any additional burdens on families.**

The means used to procure resources and services should not cause families added stress and strain. Rather, families should become more capable and competent and derive positive benefits from service coordination as part of the IFSP.

- **Service coordinators must be provided with the training necessary to learn the skills needed to work effectively with families and with professionals from other disciplines.**

The ability to empower families through service coordination will require that service coordinators acquire new and additional skills and competencies. Adequate training and continuing inservice opportunities must be developed and provided for service coordinators. Good interpersonal skills and effective communication skills, as described in Chapter Four, are essential for all service coordinators.

- **Effective service coordination practices will reflect the family-centered philosophy and conceptual framework of the IFSP.**

Service coordinator roles and service coordination practices must be implemented in ways that support and strengthen the family. The family-centered philosophy of the IFSP should be evident at all levels of practice.

Protection of Family Rights

Implementing the IFSP in ways that protect families from intrusion and coercion depends upon at least four considerations: privacy, confidentiality, full disclosure of information, and a family's right to decide about all aspects of the IFSP. These rights are guaranteed under Part H, which incorporates by reference Part B and the Family Educational Rights to Privacy Act (FERPA) {303.460(b)}. Table 11 on the following page lists the procedural safeguards that are included in Part H. A Task Force convened by the Mental Health Law Project, NEC*TAS, and the Division of Early Childhood (DEC) of the Council for Exceptional Children developed a guide book to procedural safeguards under Part H, *Strengthening the Role of Families in States' Early Intervention Systems* (Mental Health Law Project, NEC*TAS, & DEC, 1990).

Considerations:

- **Families have a right to privacy.**

The IFSP must be developed, implemented, and evaluated in ways that protect privacy at all times. Therefore, the IFSP should include only that information that a family thinks is necessary with respect to identified concerns, stated outcomes, and courses of action. Additionally, any discussions involving the IFSP should be done in ways that protect the privacy rights of families that are guaranteed by Part H.

- **All information must be held in the strictest confidence.**

No information about a child or family, written or verbal, can be shared with anyone without a family's permission and informed consent, except in very limited circumstances such as by court order or in health or safety emergencies. Special care needs to be taken to discuss with the parent(s) or legal guardian(s) which members of the program and which family members will be privy to what information, and under what conditions staff members will be involved in discussions about the IFSP. The parent(s) or guardian(s) must have final and absolute decision-making authority with respect to what IFSP information is shared and with whom.

Many families have expressed a concern about the entire IFSP being sent to other programs and agencies in response to requests for information and records. This "all or nothing" approach is not consistent with respect for family privacy and confidentiality. Instead, families should be able to choose which parts of the IFSP and other records will be shared with others outside the program.

Strategies suggested by families to allow selective sharing of the IFSP include the use of word processing to separate family outcomes and other family information from child data, or the photocopying of only the information a family wants to share and blocking out those sections the family does not want to share.

- **Full disclosure of information must be afforded to families at all times.**

Families must have full access to any and all information pertinent to the development and implementation of the IFSP. This includes assessment information, existing records, new data gathered as part of the IFSP process, etc. One important aspect of this issue is the determination by the parent(s) or legal guardian(s) of which family members will have access to such information. This determination is particularly important when legal issues within a family, such as custody or guardianship, are involved, but it is also a consideration when extended family members are involved in the IFSP process.

Table 11

Part H Procedural Safeguards

(20 USC 1480)

- The timely administrative resolution of complaints by parents, with a right to appeal.
- The right to confidentiality of personally identifiable information.
- The opportunity for parents or guardians to examine records relating to assessment, screening, eligibility, and the development and implementation of the IFSP.
- Procedures to protect the rights of the infants and toddlers if the parents or guardian of the child are not known or are unavailable or if the child is a ward of the state, including the assignment of a person to act as a surrogate for the parents.
- Written prior notice to the parents whenever the state agency or provider proposes or refuses to initiate or change the identification, evaluation, placement, or provision of appropriate early intervention services. This written notice must be in the parents' native language, unless it clearly is not feasible, and must inform parents of all the procedures they have available to them under this Section.
- During the time a proceeding or action involving a complaint is underway, unless the state agency and parents agree otherwise, the child shall continue to receive the early intervention services currently being provided or, if applying for initial services, shall receive the services not in dispute.

- **Families can invite persons of their choosing to be a part of their IFSP planning teams and should have a say in determining which professionals will be on the IFSP team.**

Although this consideration is not listed as a procedural safeguard in Part H, families do have the right to invite persons of their choosing to be part of their IFSP teams and to help determine the key players in the development and implementation of their IFSPs {303.343}. Families also should help decide who will be added to the teams as family needs change during the implementation phase of the IFSP process.

For example:

> **Vignette #2** -- The Griffin family's concerns changed after Benjamin came home. As Leslie became responsible for his daily medical care at home, she experienced a number of new stresses and needs. She was able to locate a resource in her community to help her meet those needs, her local parent-to-parent support organization. As Leslie and Michael became involved with the organization, they invited their parent-to-parent resource person to become a member of their IFSP team.

Resolving Family Concerns

If the IFSP is developed, implemented, and revised in ways that are responsive to family concerns and needs, most conflicts can be avoided. Nonetheless, dispute resolution procedures are necessary to ensure that families have an established channel of communication for resolving conflicts and voicing concerns. All staff should be familiar with conflict resolution processes, and these procedures should be discussed with each family early in its involvement with the program. The internal conflict resolution process also should be described in the program descriptions that are given to families and posted in various locations throughout the agency or program. A five-step process is discussed below. It is the responsibility of the service coordinator to help families through this process including, if necessary, referral to advocacy services such as the state protection and advocacy agency or a Parent Training and Information Center.

> **Step 1:** Proactive and responsive interventions should be used to significantly decrease the likelihood of concerns and conflicts.

Protection of Family Privacy: Considerations

- Families have a right to privacy.
- All information must be held in the strictest confidence.
- Full disclosure of information must be afforded to families at all times.
- Families can invite persons of their choosing to be a part of their IFSP planning team and should have a say in determining which professionals will be on the team.

The IFSP should be developed and implemented so that there are multiple opportunities and methods for families to provide informal and formal feedback to staff regarding their satisfaction with their IFSPs and the IFSP process. Such methods can include regular satisfaction questionnaires, a suggestion box, and an open-door policy for the director and other staff.

> **Step 2:** Families should be afforded the opportunity to voice concerns directly to the staff who are working with them so that resolution of problems can occur at this most informal level.

This will require that staff working with families learn the listening and interaction skills necessary to resolve conflict and respond to concerns without becoming defensive.

> **Step 3:** The program or agency should have an internal conflict resolution process for use in cases in which Step 2 activities do not adequately address conflicts and concerns.

Internal resolution procedures should be used, when possible, to address conflicts and concerns before any outside resolution procedures. For example, when the Johnson family were unhappy with the service they were receiving from their service coordinator, they called her supervisor to resolve the problem rather than contacting an outside resource.

Many families will want to use such an internal process to address problems and concerns with the people most directly involved. However, no internal process can or should be allowed to delay a family's right to immediate access to the formal dispute resolution process provided for in Part H and the regulations.

Step 4: If the internal process fails to resolve the problem to the family's satisfaction, the lead agency should make available a trained mediator to help the family and the program resolve their problem. Mediation, while more formal than Steps 1-3, still allows the family and the program to retain the power to make decisions to resolve the conflict.

Step 5: When all of the above steps fail to resolve conflicts, or at any time in the process that a family chooses, a formal administrative process should be used in which an impartial individual knowledgeable about Part H resolves the dispute.

When this step is necessary, the use of external resolution procedures should occur as quickly as possible to ensure that there is minimal disruption of services to the child and family.

Transagency Implementation

A major feature of quality early intervention programs is the coordination and integration of services from multiple agencies to address the needs of infants and toddlers and their families. This coordination and integration poses two unique problems with respect to the IFSP: implementation when there are multiple agencies involved in the development of the IFSP; and implementation when there are multiple service coordinators involved with the same family.

Multiple Agencies

The involvement of multiple agencies with the same family is likely to be the rule rather than the exception. In such instances, early intervention staff, particularly service coordinators, must have the skills to work effectively with staff from different agencies to facilitate the provision of resources and services to meet child and family needs. These skills include the ability to encourage staff from various agencies to work together and the ability to promote the coordinated flow of resources from multiple agencies and persons.

Multiple Service Coordinators

When separate service systems each require a service coordinator to ensure that services flow smoothly within that system, these personnel are hired to meet the bureaucratic needs of the agency, not the needs of families. When such situations do exist and when consistent with a family's choice, it is preferable that the service coordinator from the early intervention program function in a lead capacity for the IFSP. Special attention needs to be paid to the consistent transmittal of information to the family by service coordinators and the integration of information from all sources, with frequent and regular consultation between and among service coordinators.

IFSP Evaluation

The service coordinator and other members of the IFSP team are accountable for implementing the IFSP in ways that achieve stated intentions. The service coordinator is also responsible for facilitating the review and evaluation of the IFSP {303.6(b)(2)}. The following guidelines, at a minimum, should be used as a basis for evaluating IFSPs:

- **Any system of accountability must provide multiple opportunities and methods for families to evaluate the program.**

Although Part H and its accompanying regulations specify that the IFSP must be evaluated once a year and reviewed at least every six months, the Expert Team and Task Force suggested that such a schedule is not frequent enough, given the rapid changes in child and family needs and concerns during infancy and early childhood. In fact, IFSP outcomes and strategies should be informally reviewed and evaluated for appropriateness and effectiveness at every contact between a family and staff. If it is to be a living document, the IFSP must be a fluid reflection of a family's desired outcomes at any given time.

Opportunities for families to evaluate an early intervention program should be integrated into program routines. Families can evaluate specific program events, program personnel, team process, and overall satisfaction with the program. The draft IFSP form for the state of Minnesota, for example, contains an optional page that families and other members of the IFSP team can use to evaluate the IFSP team process (see Appendix E).

Simple open-ended questions asked at regular intervals during implementation can serve as an appropriate measure of program impact. Examples of such questions are "How do you think the program's involvement with your family has affected your family life?" and "What effect has the program had that you didn't anticipate?" Two sample family-centered family satisfaction measures are included in Appendix E for reference. For reliability and validity data on one of them, the *Parent Satisfaction Survey*, see Kovach and Jacks, 1989.

- **The IFSP should be evaluated in terms of both the processes used to develop and provide services and the extent to which outcomes are achieved or needs are met.**

The extent to which outcomes are achieved or needs met should be evaluated using the same measures and processes that were used to determine the needs and develop the outcomes. If, for example, an outcome was based on a father's expressed desire for more information and support, only that same father can determine if his need has been met.

A good way to evaluate a program's entire IFSP process is to compare a number of IFSPs developed within the program. If the composition of the team, the kind of outcomes and activities, and the array of service options and intensities are found to be quite similar in many of the Plans, then there may be a serious problem with that program's IFSP process.

- **Accountability should be measured in terms of a number of features and characteristics, including but not limited to flexibility, responsiveness, consumer satisfaction, and timelines.**

In their IFSP guidelines, the Parents as Partners Project in Albuquerque, New Mexico, advised other parents on the importance of parent satisfaction with IFSP progress:

> If you aren't comfortable with the way something is working (or if it's not working), discuss it with your service coordinator. Parent satisfaction is an important part of keeping track of whether goals are being met, so when the service coordinator asks you "how do you think it's going", tell . . . her. (p. 11)

Future Directions for the IFSP

By Roxane K. Kaufmann, Joicey L. Hurth, and Beverley H. Johnson

Introduction

Although the Individualized Family Service Plan is the cornerstone of family-centered early intervention, it is just one component of the statewide systems of early intervention proposed by Part H. The other minimum components of these systems provide the necessary supporting structure of interagency, interdisciplinary, and family/professional collaboration upon which the promise of the IFSP rests.

The law directs those involved in developing statewide early intervention systems to look beyond the confines of any one agency or discipline. The early intervention services that are to be provided as part of the IFSP are deliberately not described as "special education and related services." Rather, they are a diverse collection of child and family support services that are associated with education, health, mental health, and social services.

In recognition of the fact that no one discipline has primacy in the rich patchwork quilt that is the field called "early intervention," Public Law 99-457 did not assign a specific state agency to be the lead in developing the statewide system of early intervention. Instead, each state was directed to choose a lead agency and determine for itself the most judicious blend of collaborative relationships among education, health, mental health, and social services. If the IFSP provision of the law is to meet its promise to infants and toddlers with special needs and their families, local service providers must develop these same kinds of collaborative relationships with each other and with the families they serve. It is impossible for any one program or professional group to own the IFSP process in a state or in a community.

The guidelines and recommended practices for the IFSP that are presented in this document have been a good beginning for the development of family-centered IFSP processes, but they are *only* a beginning. As professionals and families have worked together on these issues, much more has been learned. It is the hope of the Expert Team and Task Force that the IFSP philosophy and conceptual framework outlined in this document will continue to provide a solid foundation for the work taking place in states and communities.

To help those involved in planning, implementing, and evaluating the IFSP component of Part H, this chapter summarizes the implications of a family-centered approach to the IFSP. All of these points are discussed throughout the document. They are gathered here to serve as a guide or checklist of things to consider for planners and policy makers, personnel training programs, service providers, and families.

Considerations for Planners and Policy Makers

A family-centered approach to the IFSP is possible only with leadership and support from planners and policy makers. Local service providers and families are looking to their state Interagency Coordinating Councils, lead agencies, and other state departments for policy statements and regulatory guidance. Traditional agency-centered approaches to the IFSP process that are designed to meet the needs of agencies rather than the people they serve are not an adequate response to this challenge.

States are currently developing and refining the written policies and procedures that will guide local implementation of Part H. The process is complex, involving both development of new policies and procedures, and interagency review and modification of previously existing ones to ensure consistency with the spirit and intent of Part H. Ensuring opportunities for public comment is also crucial to this process.

NEC*TAS, ACCH, and other members of the team contributing to this document have had many conversations with state planners about family-centered approaches to developing IFSP policy at the state level and have reviewed many states' draft policies and procedures. Although each state's policy development process has been unique, there have been interesting common approaches. The great majority of states are trying to ensure that emerging policies are consistent with family-centered principles, are broadly representative of diverse communities and perspectives, and are tested and revised based on local experience.

It may be helpful for planners and policy makers from all of the agencies providing early intervention services to consider the following action steps as they continue to develop and refine IFSP policies and procedures:

- Continue to examine current policies, regulations, and guidelines for consistency with the family-centered principles and conceptual framework described in Chapter Two and discussed throughout this document.

- Consider the rationale for any policy that seems agency-centered rather than family-centered. Can it be changed to reflect the clear intent of Part H?

- Be open to new approaches and solutions both to long-standing problems and to new IFSP concerns. Superimposing old ways on the new statewide systems might jeopardize the entire IFSP component.

- Model family/professional collaboration by involving significant numbers of parents and other family members in the planning and policy making process.

- Ensure that all policies are flexible enough to allow local programs to be responsive to individual family priorities and choices.

Remember, the IFSP is only one small piece of a comprehensive system. It is important to envision a family-centered system in its entirety.

Considerations for Training Programs

Family-centered early intervention also depends greatly on the attitudes and skills of the professionals who are participating in the IFSP process. Professionals must be willing to accept and develop new roles in their interactions with families. Preservice and inservice personnel preparation programs have a critical role to play in bringing about this willingness and ability to adopt a new approach.

Family-centered early intervention represents an opportunity for professionals and families to come together in ways that are unique to the early years of a child's life. A new or unexpected circumstance can arise every time a service provider enters a family's life. If, as a family-centered philosophy demands, respect and honesty underlie all interactions with families, professionals must learn to listen to and consult with families. In this consultant role, professionals must know how to recognize or identify both traditional and informal resources in the combination that, consistent with family choice, makes the most sense for an individual child and family.

In planning training programs to develop and supplement professional skills, states are proposing a variety of approaches, including competency-based training, early intervention certification standards, minimum inservice training requirements, and options for using paraprofessionals. The following training approaches are among those being explored:

- summer institutes;

- community colleges training consortia;
- satellite and cable TV mini courses; and
- interagency and interdisciplinary workshops.

States are also investigating how to coordinate with and make use of existing inservice training resources such University Affiliated Programs and Parent Training and Information Centers, as well as EEPCD projects, Maternal and Child Health Bureau SPRANS projects, and other projects assisting in the replication or adaptation of existing service models.

The following things to consider may be helpful to those who are training professionals to work in a family-centered fashion:

- Continue to examine current curriculum and training procedures. Are they consistent with a family-centered approach, or are they almost entirely oriented toward working with children?
- Determine the attitudes, skills, and competencies that are necessary for professionals to work with families in a family-centered, culturally competent fashion. Integrate these attitudes, skills, and competencies into the training curriculum.
- Investigate the most effective strategies and methods for teaching these attitudes and building these skills and incorporate them into the training program. For example, an assignment to provide an evening of respite care for a child with severe special needs can provide a physician-in-training with a unique opportunity to experience life from a family's perspective.
- Consider the role models available to professionals in training. Do faculty have family-centered attitudes and practices to share with trainees?
- Involve families in curriculum development and in teaching so that professionals can hear and learn directly from families. For example, the Family-Centered Institute, a personnel preparation grant to the University of Vermont Center for Developmental Disabilities and Parent-to-Parent of Vermont, employs a curriculum that was developed and is taught by both families and professionals.
- Include formal, structured opportunities for professionals to work across disciplinary and agency boundaries to encourage an interdisciplinary and interagency approach.

Families, as well as professionals may choose to develop new attitudes and skills as part of the IFSP process. Many parents and parent organizations are asking that training be made available to family members in skills such as service coordination and family/professional collaboration. Personnel preparation programs can be a resource for families, providing them with opportunities to receive training alongside early intervention professionals.

Considerations for Service Providers

In the past few years, many professionals providing early intervention services have moved steadily toward a family-centered approach. Such an approach is necessary if IFSPs are to be developed and carried out in a way that supports families' goals and choices for their children and themselves.

Although planning and policy development must occur at the state level, it is at the community level that policies and procedures come to life. Part H envisions a system of services and supports, both formal and informal, that can be configured to match the specific priorities, concerns, and choices of an individual child and family. Providers of such services and supports will be diverse and may include family members, neighbors, and paraprofessionals, as well as professionals in early intervention, health, education, mental health, and social services.

Service providers are being asked to take on new roles and to participate as part of an interagency system. They are being asked to interact in partnerships with families, to speak in everyday language that is free from professional jargon, and to act as consultants to families and to each other. Although this challenge is exciting to many professionals, it is intimidating and burdensome to others. A system of mentoring and supervision is an important support for professionals striving to become more family-centered.

The following things to consider may be helpful reminders for service providers:

- Establish an interagency work group of professionals and families to monitor local interagency implementation of the IFSP process and IFSP services. Establish communication channels to provide feedback to state planners on successful policies and procedures as well as impediments to providing family-centered services.

- Continue to examine agency and program policies and procedures. Are they consistent with the family-centered philosophy and conceptual framework outlined in this document?

- Advocate to change any policy or procedure concerning families that is agency- or professional-centered rather than family-centered.

- Examine individual practices. Do they reflect a respect for family individuality and autonomy? Do they honor the racial, ethnic, cultural, and socioeconomic diversity of families?

- Create opportunities for family/professional partnerships and collaboration.

Considerations for Families

Families occupy a unique position in the IFSP process; they are both participants in and recipients of services. All professionals working with infants and toddlers with special needs and their families are obligated to act in certain ways, but families do not have the same kinds of obligations. It is up to them to chose the level and nature of how early intervention will be involved in their lives. Therefore, there are no absolutes for families. Families may choose smaller or more expansive roles. They also may choose to extend their role on behalf of other families by participating in shaping policy or evaluating systems and services.

Families have been instrumental in shaping both the crafting of Part H and its implementation. On the federal and state levels, family members participate on the Interagency Coordinating Councils, advising and assisting the federal departments involved in early intervention and the state lead agencies in developing early intervention systems. On both the state and community levels, families are serving on task forces developing IFSP policies and procedures. Many states have hired parents as administrators and trainers. Parents are running central directories, developing family networks for advocacy, and training professionals and other family members in IFSP practices.

The following considerations may be helpful to families as they consider their role options:

- Seek information about available systems, services, and processes.

- Ask questions, and ask for explanations of any answers that aren't clear.

- Choose the role options that match family values, goals, hopes, and concerns.

- Ask for training that supports chosen roles.

- Work toward partnerships with the professionals who are part of the IFSP process.

- Work with parent members of the federal and state Interagency Coordinating Councils to help them represent the views of families in the state and in the nation.

Conclusion

As state planners and policy makers, families, and professionals enter into partnerships to implement Part H, it is helpful to remember that Public Law 99-457 was just the beginning of a process. The law by itself cannot change practice. Moving toward family-centered systems of early intervention requires a vision and a willingness of agencies and institutions to change.

Unfortunately, institutions are often characterized by inertia. This inertia can be carried forward by the attitudes of individuals at various levels throughout the system -- from receptionists, to managers, to auditors -- and through the day-to-day rules, regulations, and other formal and informal structures of agencies and institutions. These can conspire to construct real barriers both to the provision of services and the active participation of families in the system. It is up to families and professionals, working together, to translate the clear intent of the law into early intervention systems and programs that are open and flexible, truly representing family-centered principles and practices (D. A. Jones, personal communication, February 1991).

The Individualized Family Service Plan component of the law, if implemented in a manner consistent with the family-centered philosophy and conceptual framework described in this monograph, can serve as a model for making family-centered early intervention services a reality for all infants and toddlers with special needs and their families.

Glossary

Assessment Planning -- the gathering and exchange of information between family members and providers that shape the assessment process.

Best Practice for the IFSP -- a judgment, based on the consensus of providers, family members, policy-makers, and advocates, that this IFSP process is effective and meets the highest standards of clinical excellence and family-centered principles.

Child Assessment -- the collection and synthesis of information from those who are familiar with the child, as well as the seeking of new information for purposes of identifying the child's strengths, needs, the nature and cause of problems, and recommendations for remediation. In this document, the term "child assessment" is used instead of evaluation or testing.

Empowerment -- the interaction of professionals with families in such a way that families maintain or acquire a sense of control over their family lives and attribute positive changes that result from early intervention to their own strengths, abilities, and actions.

Enabling -- creating opportunities and means for families to display their present abilities and competencies and to acquire new ones that are necessary to meet the needs of their children and themselves.

Family's Agenda -- a family's priorities and choices for its child and itself that determine how early intervention will be involved in family life.

Family Concerns -- areas that family members identify as needs, issues, or problems they want to address as part of the IFSP process.

Family Priorities -- a family's agenda and choices for how early intervention will be involved in family life.

Family Resources -- the strengths, abilities, and formal and informal supports that can be mobilized to meet family concerns, needs, or outcomes.

Family Strengths -- characteristics that family members identify as contributing to the growth and development of the child and family. Among the areas of family life that many families identify as strengths are coping strategies, nurturing relationships, communication, religious or personal beliefs, family competence, and family/community interconnectedness.

Family-Centered -- the recognition that the family is the constant in a child's life and that service systems and personnel must support, respect, encourage, and enhance the strength and competence of the family.

IFSP Evaluation -- the determination of the appropriateness and effectiveness of the IFSP process, outcomes, and services.

IEP Goals and Objectives -- the long- and short-term behaviors that are the targets of special education or therapeutic intervention. IEP objectives are almost always written in behavioral terms.

IFSP Outcomes -- statements of the changes families wants to see for their children or themselves.

IFSP Team -- the family members and professionals who meet together to assess the child, identify family strengths and needs, develop and carry out outcomes and strategies, and evaluate the effectiveness of the IFSP.

Normalization Principle -- the principle that children and families should have access to services provided in as usual a fashion and environment as possible. Normalization helps the child and family become or remain part of their community.

Screening -- a process of identifying those children who appear to have early intervention needs and recommending further investigation or referral.

Service Coordination (Case Management) -- an active process for implementing the IFSP that promotes and supports a family's capacities and competencies to identify, obtain, coordinate, monitor, and evaluate resources and services to meet its needs.

References

Early Intervention Program for Infants and Toddlers with Handicaps; Final Regulations, 34 CFR 303. (1989, June 22). *Federal Register, 54*(119), 26306-26348.

Education of Handicapped Act Amendments of 1986 (P.L. 99-457), 20 U.S.C. Secs. 1400-1485 (1986).

Individuals with Disabilities Education Act (P.L. 100-476), 20 U.S.C. Secs. 1400-1485 (1990).

Alexander, R., & Tompkins-McGill, P. (1987). Notes to the experts from the parent of a handicapped child. *Social Work, 32*(4), 361-362.

Aponte, H. (1986). "If I don't get simple, I cry." *Family Process, 25*(4), 531-548.

Bailey, D. B. (1984). A triaxial model of the interdisciplinary team and group process. *Exceptional Children, 51*(1), 17-25.

Bailey, D. B. (1987). Collaborative goal setting with families: Resolving differences in values and priorities for services. *Topics in Early Childhood Special Education, 7*(2), 59-71.

Bailey, D. B. (1988). Considerations in developing family goals. In D. B. Bailey & R. J. Simeonsson (Eds.), *Family assessment in early intervention* (pp. 229-249). Columbus, OH: Charles E. Merrill.

Bailey, D. B. (in press). Issues and perspectives on family assessment. *Infants and Young Children.*

Bailey, D., & Blasco, P. (1990). Parents' perspectives on a written survey of family needs. *Journal of Early Intervention, 14*(3), 196-203.

Bailey, D. B., Winton P. J., Rouse, L., & Turnbull, A. P. (1989). Family goals in infant intervention: Analysis and issues. *Journal of Early Intervention, 14*(1), 15-26.

Black, T., Prestridge, S., & Anderson, J. (1981). *The development of a needs assessment process.* Chapel Hill, NC: Technical Assistance Development System.

Blechert, T., Christiansen, M., & Kari, N. (1987). Intraprofessional team building. *American Journal of Occupational Therapy, 41*(9), 576-582.

Brown, W. (1990). *Early intervention regulation: Annotation and analysis of Part H.* Horsham, PA: LRP Publications.

Cecchin, G. (1987). Hypothesizing, circularity, and neutrality revisited: An invitation to curiosity. *Family Process, 26*(4), 405-414.

Cross, T. L. (1988). Cultural competence continuum. *Focal Point, 3*(1), 1-4.

Davis, P., & Kaufmann, R. K. (1990, February). *Identifying family strengths and needs.* Paper presented at the LRP Publications Conference on Early Intervention and Preschool, Alexandria, VA.

Deal, A. G., Dunst, C. J., & Trivette, C. M. (1989). A flexible and functional approach to developing Individualized Family Support Plans. *Infants and Young Children, 1*(4), 32-43.

DiVenere, N. J. (1988, November). *The development and management of Individualized Family Service Plans: The family perspective.* Paper presented at the American Academy of Pediatrics Meeting on Public Law 99-457, Washington, DC.

Dokecki, P. R., & Heflinger, C. A. (1989). Strengthening families of young handicapped children with handicapping conditions: Mapping backward from the "street level." In J. J. Gallagher, P. L. Trohanis, & R. M. Clifford (Eds.), *Policy implementation and PL 99-457: Planning for young children with special needs* (pp. 59-84). Baltimore: Paul H. Brookes.

Dunst, C. J. (1985). Rethinking early intervention. *Analysis and Intervention in Developmental Disabilities, 5*, 165-201.

Dunst, C. J. (1987, December). *What is effective helping?* Paper presented at the Fifth Biennial National Training Institute of the National Center for Clinical Infant Programs, Washington, DC.

Dunst, C. J. (1988). Assessing handicapped infants and toddlers and their families [Special issue]. *Society of Pediatric Psychology/Newsletter, 12*(3), 7-9.

Dunst, C. J. (1990). Family support principles: Checklists for program builders and practitioners. *Family Systems Intervention Monograph Series, 2*, No. 5, Morganton, NC: Family, Infant and Preschool Program, Western Carolina Center.

Dunst, C. J., & Paget, K. D. (in press). Parent-professional partnerships and family empowerment. In M. Fine & C. Carlson (Eds.), *Handbook of home-school intervention: A systems perspective*. Boston: Allyn and Bacon.

Dunst, C. J., & Trivette, C. M. (1987). Enabling and empowering families: Conceptual and intervention issues. *School Psychology Review, 16*(4), 443-456.

Dunst, C. J., Leet, H. E., & Trivette, C. M. (1988). Family resources, personal well-being, and early intervention. *Journal of Special Education, 22*, 108-116.

Dunst, C. J., Trivette, C., & Deal, A. (1988). *Enabling and empowering families: Principles and guidelines for practice*. Cambridge, MA: Brookline Books.

Dunst, C. J., Trivette, C. M., Gordon, N. J., & Pletcher, L. L. (1989). Building and mobilizing informal family support networks. In G. Singer & L. Irvin (Eds.), *Support for caregiving families* (pp. 121-141). Baltimore: Paul H. Brookes.

Edelman, L. (1991). *Recognizing family-centered care: A group exercise*. Baltimore: The Kennedy Institute.

Edwards, D. (1989, May). *Culture, socioeconomic status, and children with AIDS*. Paper presented at the 24th Annual Conference of the Association for the Care of Children's Health, Anaheim, CA.

Fewell, R. R. (1983). The team approach to infant education. In S. G. Garwood & R. R. Fewell (Eds.), *Educating handicapped infants: Issues in development and intervention* (pp. 299-322). Rockville, MD: Aspen.

Foster, M., Berger, M., & McLean, M. (1981). Rethinking a good idea: A reassessment of parent involvement. *Topics in Early Childhood Special Education, 1*(3), 55-56.

Garland, C. W., Osborne, S., & Buck, D. M. (1988). *Process model for clarifying values in early intervention.* Lightfoot, VA: Child Development Resources.

Garland, C. W., Woodruff, G., & Buck, D. M. (1988, June). *Case Management*. (Available from Division for Early Childhood of the Council for Exceptional Children, 1920 Association Drive, Reston, VA 22091).

Gilkerson, L., Hilliard, A. G., Schrag, E., & Shonkoff, J. (1987). *Report accompanying the education of the handicapped act amendments (Report #99-860) and comments on P.L. 99-457.* Washington, DC: National Maternal and Child Health Clearinghouse.

Hanson, M. J., Lynch, E. W., & Wayman, I. I. (1990). Honoring the cultural diversity of families when gathering data. *Topics in Early Childhood Special Education, 10*(1), 112-131.

Hartman, A. (1981). The family: A central focus for practice. *Social Work, 26*, 7-13.

Healy, A., Keesee, P. D., & Smith, B. S. (1989). *Early services for children with special needs: Transactions for family support.* Baltimore: Paul H. Brookes.

Hobbs, N., Dokecki, P. R., Hoover-Dempsey, K. V., Moroney, R. M., Shayne, M. W., & Weeks, K. H. (1984). *Strengthening families*. San Francisco: Jossey-Bass.

House Memorial 5 Task Force on Young Children and Families. (1990, November 6). *First steps to a community based, coordinated continuum of care for New Mexico children and families.* (Available from Polly Arango, P.O. Box 338, Algodones, NM 87001).

Howard, J. (1982). The role of the pediatrician with young exceptional children and their families. *Exceptional Children, 48*(4), 316-322.

Hunt, M., Cornelius, P., Leventhal, P., Miller, P., Murray, T., & Stoner, G. (1990). *Into our lives.* Akron, OH: Children's Hospital Medical Center.

Johnson, B. H., McGonigel, M. J., & Kaufmann, R. K. (1989). *Guidelines and recommended practices for the Individualized Family Service Plan.* Washington, DC: Association for the Care of Children's Health.

Jones, D. A. (1988). Cultural perspectives on health. In D. A. Jones (Ed.), *Cultural perspectives on health: The mini-series on ethnic minorities* (pp. 1-9). Unpublished monograph. University of Wisconsin-Madison, Waisman Center on Mental Retardation and Developmental Disabilites, Madison.

Kjerland, L. (1986). *Early intervention tailor made.* Eagan, MN: Project Dakota, Inc.

Kjerland, L., & Kovach, J. (1987). *Structures for program responsiveness to parents*. Eagan, MN: Project Dakota, Inc.

Kovach, J. (1986). *Project Dakota final report (1983-1986).* Eagan, MN: Project Dakota, Inc.

Kovach, J., & Jacks, R. (1989). *Program evaluation using the Project Dakota Parent Satisfaction Survey*. Eagan, MN: Dakota, Inc.

Leviton, A., Mueller, M., & Kauffman, C. (1991). *The family-centered catalytic consultation model: Practical applications for professionals*. Unpublished manuscript. The Kennedy Institute, Baltimore.

Linder, T. (1987). *Early childhood special education: Program development and administration*. Baltimore: Paul H. Brookes.

May, J. (1991). *Fathers of children with special needs: New horizons*. Bethesda, MD: Association for the Care of Children's Health.

McGonigel, M. (1990, April). *A family-centered process for the Individualized Family Service Plan.* Paper presented at the Third Annual Early Intervention Conference, University of Connecticut Health Science Center, Cromwell, CT.

McGonigel, M. J., & Garland, C. (1988). The individualized family service plan and the early intervention team: Team and family issues and recommended practices. *Infants and Young Children, 1*(1), 10-21.

Meisels, S. J., & Provence, S. (1989). *Screening and assessment: Guidelines for identifying young disabled and developmentally vulnerable children and their families*. Washington, DC: National Center Clinical Infant Programs.

Mental Health Law Project, NEC*TAS, & DEC. (1990). *Strengthening the role of families in states' early intervention systems*. Washington, DC and Reston, VA: MHLP and DEC.

National Center for Family-Centered Care. (1990). *What is family-centered care?* (brochure). Washington, DC: Association for the Care of Children's Health.

Parents as Partners Project. (1988). *Preparing for the Individualized Family Service Plan (IFSP)*. Albuquerque, NM: Alta Mira Specialized Family Services, Inc.

Peterson, N. (1987). *Early intervention for handicapped and at-risk children: An introduction to early childhood special education*. Denver: Love Publishing.

Place, P. (1989). *Status of the states' progress toward developing a policy concerning the development of the Individualized Family Service Plan.* Chapel Hill, NC: Carolina Policy Studies Program, University of North Carolina at Chapel Hill.

Rappaport, J. (1984). Studies in empowerment: Introduction to the issues. In J. Rappaport, C. Swift, & R. Hess (Eds.), *Studies in empowerment: Steps toward understanding and action*. (pp. 1-37). New York: Haworth Press.

Regional Research Institute for Human Services. (1987, Winter). Portland hosts parent/ professional collaboration training session. *Focal Point 2*(2), 1-3.

Richardson, B. B. (1979). Human service delivery for high risk infants. In *An Ecological Model of Services to Inner City Minority Handicapped Infants*. (pp. 12-16). Los Angeles: Charles R. Drew Medical School.

Roberts, R. (1990). *Developing culturally competent programs for families of children with special needs* (2nd ed.). Washington, DC: Georgetown Child Development Center.

Shelton, T., Jeppson, E., & Johnson, B. (1987). *Family-centered care for children with special health care needs*. Washington, DC: Association for the Care of Children's Health.

Stoneman, Z. (1985). Family involvement in early childhood special education programs. In N.H. Fallen & W. Umansky (Eds.), *Young children with special needs* (2nd ed.) (pp. 442-469). Columbus, OH: Charles E. Merrill.

Summers, J. A., Dell'Oliver, C., Turnbull, A. P., Benson, H., Santelli, E., Campbell, M., Siegel-Causey, E. (1990). Examining the Individualized Family Service Plan process: What are family and practitioner preferences? *Topics in Early Childhood Special Education, 10*(1), 78-99.

Tomm, K. (1987). Interventive interviewing: Part II. Reflexive questioning as a means to enable self-healing. *Family Process, 26*(2), 167-184.

Trivette, C. M., Deal, A., & Dunst, C. J. (1986). Family needs, sources of support, and professional roles: Critical elements of family systems assessment and intervention. *Diagnostique, 11*, 146-267.

Trivette, C. M., Dunst, C. J., Deal, A. G., Hamer, A. W., & Propst, S. (1990). Assessing family strengths and family functioning style. *Topics in Early Childhood Special Education, 10*(1), 16-35.

Turnbull, A., Lee, I., & Turbiville, V. (1991). *IFSP process model*. Unpublished manuscript. University of Kansas, Beach Center on Families and Disability, Lawrence.

Turnbull, A. P., Blue-Banning, M., Behr, S., & Kerns, G. (1986). Family research and intervention: A value and ethical examination. In P. Dokecki & R. Zaner (Eds.), *Ethics and decision-making for persons with severe handicaps: Toward an ethically relevant research agenda*. Baltimore: Paul H. Brookes.

Turnbull, A. P., & Summers, J. A. (1985, April). *From family involvement to family support: Evolution to revolution*. Paper presented at the Down Syndrome State-of-the-Art Conference, Boston.

Turnbull, A. P., & Turnbull, H. R. (1986). *Families, professionals, and exceptionality: A special partnership*. Columbus, OH: Charles E. Merrill.

Turnbull, H. R., Guess, D., & Turnbull, A. P. (1988). Vox populi and Baby Doe. *Mental Retardation, 26*, 127-132.

Vincent, L. (1990). *Addressing families' concerns/strengths through the IFSP*. Paper presented at Third Annual Early Intervention Conference, Children's Hospital Medical Center, Akron, OH

Vincent, L. (1988). What we have learned from families. *OSERS News in Print, 1*(4), 3.

Wayman, K. I., Lynch, E. W., & Hanson, M. J. (1990). Home-based early childhood services: Cultural sensitivity in a family systems approach. *Topics in Early Childhood Special Education, 10*(4), 56-75.

Weinstein, V. (1979). An ecological model for intervention with inner-city poor and/or minority handicapped infants and their families: The Community. In *An Ecological Model of Services to Inner City Minority Handicapped Infants* (pp. 27-29). Los Angeles: Charles R. Drew Medical School.

Winton, P. J. (1988). Effective communication between parents and professionals. In D. B. Bailey & R. J. Simeonsson (Eds.), *Family assessment in early intervention* (pp. 207-228). Columbus, OH: Charles E. Merrill.

Winton, P. J., & Bailey, D. B. (1988). The family focused interview: A collaborative mechanism for family assessment and goal setting. *Journal of the Division for Early Childhood, 12*(3), 195-207.

Winton, P. J., & Bailey, D. B. (1990). Early intervention training related to family interviewing. *Journal of Early Intervention, 14*(1), 50-62.

Woodruff, G., & McGonigel, M. J. (1988). Early intervention team models: The transdisciplinary approach. In J. J. Gallagher, P. Hutinger, J. B. Jordan, & M. B. Karnes (Eds.), *Early childhood special education: Birth to three*. Reston, VA: Council for Exceptional Children.

Woodruff, G., Hanson, C. R., McGonigel, M., & Sterzin, E. D. (1990). *Community-based services for children with HIV infection and their families: A manual for planners, service providers, families, & advocates*. Brighton, MA: South Shore Mental Health Center.

Woodruff, G., McGonigel, M., Garland, C., Zeitlin, S., Chazkel-Hochman, J., Shanahan, K., Toole, A., & Vincent, L. (1985). *Planning programs for infants* (State Series Paper No. 2). Chapel Hill, NC: Technical Assistance Development System, University of North Carolina at Chapel Hill. (ERIC Document Reproduction Service No. ED 266 573).

Appendix A: Sample IFSPs

Sample Individualized Family Service Plan #1

The Crowder Family

(See vignette #1, Chapter Three, pages 25-26)

The IFSP for the Crowder family was developed by Geneva Woodruff and Chris Hanson at Project WIN in Roxbury, Massachusetts, with assistance from Ibby Jeppson and Mary McGonigel of ACCH and Patti Place of NASDSE. The format for this IFSP was developed by Roxane Kaufmann of NEC*TAS and Mary McGonigel and Josie Thomas of ACCH to provide a simple form that includes all the Part H requirements, yet is still "family friendly." This IFSP would have been handwritten to emphasize the informality and flexibility that should characterize IFSPs, but it was necessary to type it for reproduction clarity.

A family with a child who is HIV positive was included in this document to illustrate that some children and families will require services that go beyond those traditionally associated with early intervention and to highlight the collaboration and coordination among agencies that is critical if Part H is to fulfill its promise to these children and families. The transagency model developed at Project WIN is an approach that has proven effective in meeting the multiple needs of families whose children are HIV positive in a way that is respectful of family values and that builds on the strengths and resources already present in families.

Individualized Family Service Plan (IFSP)

Child's Name: Mary Crowder

Birthdate: 10/10/88 **Age:** 23 months

Developmental Levels:

15-18	months	Fine Motor	12-15	months	Gross Motor
15-18	months	Cognitive	18-21	months	Language
12-15	months	Self-Help	18-21	months	Social/Emotional

Vision within normal limits

Hearing within normal limits

Child Strengths and Needs:

Mary's developmental strengths are in her ability to communicate and interact with her mother, aunt, and brother and sister. Despite her many health problems, Mary's temperament is sunny, and her disposition makes it easy for her to get the adults around her involved with her.

Mary's physical health varies considerably as a result of her AIDS, and this affects her motor development, which is very uneven. Mary has persistent diarrhea and recurring ear infections. Mary is a fussy eater and sometimes throws food she doesn't like or want. She doesn't have many opportunities to play with or be around other young children, which would allow her to make the most of her good language and social skills.

Name: The Crowder Family

Family Concerns, Priorities, and Resources:

Theresa is deeply committed to keeping her family together and to caring for Mary at home as long as she can. Theresa's periods of being sick with AIDs make it hard for her, at times, to manage the demands of taking care of Mary. She has a lot of help from Yvonne and Julie, both of whom are great sources of support and can be relied on to help out whenever they are needed. Yvonne goes grocery shopping for the family, helps Julie with her school work, takes Mary and Theresa to medical appointments, and has made a home for Roger with her family. Because Theresa relies so heavily on Yvonne and because Yvonne disapproves of Theresa's drug use so strongly, Theresa wants to enter a treatment program again.

Julie is devoted to her little sister and helps out with her every chance she gets. Julie says she wants to be a very important part of Mary's IFSP team. Theresa praises Julie for her help, but she is also concerned about putting too many burdens on her. Theresa is also worried about the effect her and Mary's illness has on Julie, but Theresa says she has a hard time bringing that up with Julie.

Right now, mealtimes are not good times at the Crowders.' Theresa is often too tired to cook dinner and then coax Mary to eat, but she worries about Mary not getting enough to eat and wants to see her grow stronger. Julie manages dinner whenever Theresa is too tired, but she isn't sure what she can make for dinner that Mary would like and want to eat. Theresa also wants some time alone during the day to rest when she isn't feeling strong, and she hopes Mary will have a chance to be around other young children. Theresa needs a stroller in order for her to be able to take Mary out of the house.

Outcomes:

1. Theresa wants to control her drug use so that she can keep her good relationship with her sister.

2. Theresa wants Mary to be in child care, so that Theresa has some time to rest during the day and so that Mary can have chance to play with children her own age.

3. Theresa and Julie want some help with mealtimes so that Mary can learn how to eat more foods, be less fussy, and grow stronger.

4. Mary will have physical therapy in order to help prevent loss of her previously attained motor skills and to try to build her body strength and mobility to make it possible for Theresa and Julie to keep taking care of her at home.

5. Theresa wants Julie to have someone outside the family to talk to so that Julie can get the information and support that she needs.

Name: The Crowder Family

Outcome: # 1

Theresa wants to control her drug use so that she can keep her good relationship with her sister.

Strategies/Activities:

1. Theresa, Lizzie (the WIN service coordinator), and Lucy (Theresa's hospital social worker) will discuss Theresa's options for a drug treatment program.
2. Theresa will choose the option she prefers and will call to arrange things within a week of the discussion.
3. If there is a waiting list, Lucy will arrange for Theresa to have priority admission status because of her illness.
4. Theresa will complete the intake process for the treatment option she chooses and will go to treatment sessions as scheduled. Lizzie or Lucy will go with Theresa to her appointments whenever she asks.
5. Lucy, Lizzie, and Yvonne will help and support Theresa, encouraging her efforts. Theresa will tell Lizzie and Lucy when she feels like using drugs, and they will tell Theresa whenever they think she is using drugs.

Criteria/Timelines:

Theresa will determine if she is making progress overcoming her drug addiction. She suggested that she review her progress with Lizzie every two weeks.

Name: The Crowder Family

Outcome: # 2

Theresa wants Mary to be in child care, so that Theresa has some time to rest during the day and so that Mary can have a chance to play with children her own age.

Strategies/Activities:

1. Lizzie and Julie will investigate child care centers within walking distance of the Crowder's house and will talk over the options with Theresa within the next two weeks.
2. Theresa will make a choice from the options, after talking it over with Julie to see what program Julie thinks is best.
3. If the publicly funded child care centers are not available or if they are not appropriate for Mary, Lucy will arrange for Theresa to get financial assistance from the Department of Social Services or arrange for the hospital pediatric AIDS support program to pay the fees.
4. Lizzie and Theresa will enroll Mary together, as soon as possible.
5. Yvonne will try to get a friend to loan Theresa a stroller. If this doesn't work out in the next week, Lucy will ask Social Services to buy a stroller so that Mary can go to child care.
6. Theresa will take Mary every morning to the center when she is well enough to take her. Julie will pick Mary up in the afternoons.
7. Lizzie will arrange right away for a home health aide or visiting nurse to help out with Mary during the day when Mary is ill at home and Theresa is not well enough to manage alone. The home health aide will be paid for by the county health department.
8. When Theresa and Mary are both well, Theresa will take Mary in her stroller to the park once a week.

Criteria/Timelines:

The timelines are as listed above in the activities. Theresa will decide if she is satisfied with the way things are going and if her need has been met as specified in the outcome.

Name: The Crowder Family

Outcome: # 3

Theresa and Julie want some help with mealtimes so that Mary can learn how to eat more foods, be less fussy, and grow stronger.

Strategies/Activities:

1. Lizzie will arrange for a home nutritionist or visiting nurse to come to the Crowder's home five evenings a week, beginning in two weeks. The home visitor will be paid for by the hospital pediatric AIDS program.

2. The home visitor will help Theresa and Julie make a list of several finger foods that are good for Mary and that she likes and is able to eat.

3. The home visitor will show Julie how to make several easy-to-prepare dishes that Mary likes and is able to eat.

4. Anna Martinez, the WIN occupational therapist, and Lizzie will do a feeding evaluation of Mary next week, before the home visitor comes. They will do an assessment to determine if Mary has any special feeding problems and will develop a plan with Theresa for remediation, which will become a part of this IFSP, if necessary. The evaluation will be done at home at a regular mealtime.

5. Yvonne will continue to do the grocery shopping for the Crowders, now using a list that Julie has made for her.

Criteria/Timelines:

The timelines are as listed above in the activities. Theresa will decide if she is satisfied with the way things are going and if her need has been met as specified in the outcome.

Name: The Crowder Family

Outcome: # 4

Mary will have physical therapy in order to help prevent loss of her previously attained motor skills and to try to build her body strength and mobility to make it possible for Theresa and Julie to keep taking care of her at home.

Strategies/Activities:

1. Virginia Taylor, the hospital physical therapist, will visit Theresa and Mary at home once a week, starting next week, to monitor Mary's motor development for signs of loss of previously attained skills. Virginia's service will be paid for by the hospital pediatric HIV program.

2. Virginia will work with Mary on her balance. She will show Julie and Theresa how to play with Mary in ways that help Mary practice her balance.

3. When Julie plays with Mary, she will play in the ways that Virginia is teaching her.

4. Lizzie will come to one of Virginia's sessions every month, starting next month, to learn how Mary is doing and to be able to help Julie and Theresa play with Mary in ways that help Mary maintain her skills or grow stronger.

Criteria/Timelines:

Mary's therapy will begin next week. Virginia will use clinical observation to judge Mary's progress or Mary's maintenance of previously attained motor skills, and will do a formal evaluation of Mary jointly with Lizzie every three months to monitor Mary's motor development.

Name: The Crowder Family

Outcome: # 5

Theresa wants Julie to have someone outside the family to talk to so that Julie can get the information and support that she needs.

Strategies/Activities:

1. Julie will visit Lucy at her office once every two weeks, starting next week, so that they can talk about whatever is on Julie's mind. Lucy's services will be paid for by the hospital pediatric AIDS program.

2. In two weeks, Theresa, Lucy, and Julie will visit the support group for brothers and sisters at the hospital. If Julie likes the group, she will start attending the monthly support group sessions, and she will participate in the other group activities.

3. Theresa will let Lucy know if she has similar concerns about Roger.

Criteria/Timelines:

Theresa and Julie will decide if they are satisfied with the way things are going and if the need has been met.

Name: The Crowder Family

Other Services:

Theresa wants Mary to continue to have her health monitored at the local health clinic where both Theresa and Mary receive their primary care. Staff from the clinic are part of the Crowder's transagency team at Theresa's request.

Theresa wants Mary to continue to receive care from the AIDS program at the hospital where both Theresa and Mary receive their AIDS specialty care. The care coordinator from the AIDS program participates on the Crowder's transagency team at Theresa's request.

Notes on the IFSP Process:

Lucy Crawford, Theresa's hospital social worker, referred Theresa and Mary to Project WIN. The WIN assessment staff planned a transdisciplinary arena assessment with Theresa, Yvonne, and Julie. Lucy became part of the team for the assessment.

Following the assessment, Theresa decided to enroll in Project WIN with Mary. Lucy is part of Theresa's IFSP team, along with the occupational and physical therapists from the project. Yvonne and Julie are on the team, and Lizzie O'Shea will work with Theresa as her service coordinator.

Because Theresa and Mary have AIDS, they may need the services of many agencies other than the hospital and Project WIN. New members will be added to this transagency IFSP team by Theresa, or with Theresa's consent, as the need arises.

Theresa was very clear about the kinds of support she needed and plans to tell Lizzie any time she needs or wants a change in the IFSP for Mary, Julie, Roger, or herself. Because Yvonne may need to take over for Theresa at any time should she become too ill to care for her family, Theresa has asked that Yvonne be a full member of the team and have access to all the records relating to Mary and the Crowders' IFSP.

Back Cover Sheet–IFSP

Project WIN

Child's Name: Mary Crowder **Birthdate:** 10/10/88

Address: 1715 NE Adams Street, #527

Boston, MA **Phone:** 462-4347

Service Coordinator (Case Manager): Lizzie O'Shea, R.N.

IFSP Team Members and Signatures:

Theresa Crowder, mother	Theresa Crowder
Julie Crowder, sister	Julie Crowder
Yvonne Baker, aunt	Yvonne Baker, aunt
Lucy Crawford, M.S.W.	Lucy Crawford
Virginia Taylor, L.P.T.	Virginia Taylor, LPT
Anna Martinez, O.T.R.	Anna Martinez

Frequency, Intensity, and Duration of Services:

Services will begin immediately and continue until the September after Mary's third birthday when she is eligible for public school preschool. Frequency and intensity will vary; see individual outcomes.

IFSP Review Dates: 12/15/90 6/15/91

3/15/91 9/15/91

Transition Plan: X **Not Applicable** ______ **Yes, (see outcomes)**

Parent Signature(s):

This plan represents our wishes. I (we) understand and agree with it, and I (we) authorize Project KAI to carry out this plan with me (us).

Theresa Crowder
Parent(s)

9/15/90
Date

Sample Individualized Family Service Plan # 2

The Griffin Family

(See vignette #2, Chapter Three, pages 26-27)

The IFSP for the Griffin family was written by Nancy DiVenere of Parent-to-Parent of Vermont, Inc., with assistance from Roxane Kaufmann and Joicey Hurth of NEC*TAS and Mary McGonigel at ACCH. The form used for this IFSP was adapted from a form initially developed by the Family Child Learning Center at Children's Hospital Medical Center of Akron, Philippa Campbell, Director. The form illustrates one approach to IFSP formats, that of listing family strengths and needs individually for each outcome. The evaluation rating scale included in this IFSP is from Deal, Dunst, & Trivette, (1989).

To illustrate the need to change services as family needs and circumstances change, Nancy DiVenere deliberately included a problem in this IFSP -- the Plan was too ambitious as initially written and asked too much of Leslie. Not until the Griffins began to live with their IFSP did Leslie realize that it was requiring too much of her time in travel. She also began to feel overburdened by her responsibility for Ben's therapy. The IFSP team in this sample solved the problem by developing new, more creative approaches to Ben's therapy and by increasing the support Leslie received from her husband and from the home visitor.

*Individualized Family Service Plan**
(IFSP)

Family Name: Griffin

Child's Name: Benjamin Griffin

Address: 127 Aspen Lane
Mountain

Birthdate: 1/5/90

Phone: 729-0631

Referral Date: 6/1/90

Coordinator: Pat White, MD

By Whom: NICU

Assessment: 5/90 and 6/90

IFSP Team and Signatures:

Leslie Griffin 6/7/90
Parent or Guardian **Date**

Michael Griffin 6-7-90
Parent or Guardian **Date**

Pat White MD

Neal Gold MD

Kylie Talbot, LPT

Adrienne Wales, OTR

Amanda Grey, M.S.

[illegible signature]

Early Intervention Services (Frequency and Intensity)

Family Information and Support -- with each visit to the NICU, as specified in the activities.

PT and OT Evaluation and Monitoring -- twice weekly during Ben's hospitalization.

After Discharge:

Physical therapy once a week;
Occupational therapy once a week;
Once a week home visits from the early intervention specialist.

Other Services

None

Transition Plan Attached: ____ Yes X Not Applicable

Child's Name: Benjamin Griffin

Date: 6/7/90

Family Members/Social Supports:

	Relationship
Leslie	mother
Michael	father
Caroline	sister
Heather	neighbor

Child's Present Levels of Development:

Ben is alert and responds preferentially to his mother. He is becoming more able to tolerate being touched and to comfort himself. (For more information, see Assessment Report).

Domain	Age Level	Age Range
Cognitive	2-3 months	0-3 months
Fine Motor	2-3 months	0-3 months
Gross Motor	2-3 months	0-4 months
Language	1-2 months	0-3 months
Self-Help	0-1 month	0-1 month
Social/Emotional	0-2 months	1-2 months
Vision	within normal limits	
Hearing	within normal limits	

Child's Health Status:

Ben's health is stabilizing. He is responding well to a reduction of his oxygen levels, and plans are being made to discharge Ben in about a month if his good progress continues.

Other Agencies Involved:

Agency	Contact Person	Phone
Mountain Early Intervention Program	Kathleen Sanford	891-7026
Pulmonary Clinic	Dale Peavy	787-9576
Mountain Medical Supply, Inc.	Alice Strickland	891-2514

Child's Name: Benjamin Griffin
Date: 6/7/90

Outcome # 1:

Leslie wants to be more secure in her ability to care for Ben at home.

Identified By: Leslie

Family Concerns, Priorities, and Resources for This Outcome:

Although I have formal training in child development and an older child, I worry that I don't know enough about Ben's needs to take care of him at home. I am sure that Michael and I can read professional literature to learn by ourselves, and we can learn from the medical team at the hospital and from the experiences of the other parents. We have many friends who have volunteered to help us in any way they can, but I'm not sure what to ask them for. What I really need is to be confident that when Ben comes home, I'll know what to do. (Leslie)

Service/Action	Dates and Evaluations		
	Begin	**Review**	**End**
1. Leslie will spend some time during each visit to the nursery holding and feeding Ben.	6/9/90	7/8/90	#7 7/8/90
2. Ben's neonatalogist and his primary nurse will help Leslie recognize and read Ben's cues and find ways to soothe and comfort him.	6/9/90	7/8/90	#7 7/8/90
3. Ben's primary nurse and the other unit nurses will help Leslie assume as much of Ben's care as she wants to while he is in the nursery.	6/9/90	7/8/90	#7 7/8/90
4. Leslie and Michael are attending the NICU parent-to-parent support group and will continue after Ben is discharged, as long as they want to go. They plan to bring up their fears about taking Ben home at the next meeting. The Griffins will ask the other families about ways these families have used their friends for support and assistance.	Already Begun	Continuing	#7

Child's Name: Benjamin Griffin
Date: 6/7/90

Service/Action	Dates and Evaluations		
	Begin	Review	End
5. The medical team and the hospital infant development specialist will give the Griffins resource materials about the needs and behaviors of preemies.	6/9/90	7/8/90	7/8/90

Criteria/Timeline:

These activities will begin immediately and continue throughout Ben's hospitalization. Leslie will determine whether or not her need has been met, in consultation with Dr. White.

Child's Name: Benjamin Griffin
Date: 6/7/90

Outcome # 2:

The Griffins want help learning to take care of Ben's medical needs and finding resources in their community before Ben comes home from the hospital.

Identified By: Leslie and Michael

Family Concerns, Priorities, and Resources for This Outcome:

We need help and support to bring Ben home. We want someone to help us translate what we've learned at the hospital into routines we can use to take care of Ben at home. We have a neighbor, Heather, who has volunteered to help me with Ben. We want to learn how to teach Heather the medical care procedures for Ben. (Leslie)

I can't spend as much time at the hospital as Leslie can, but I want to be part of Ben's care. (Michael)

Service/Action	Dates and Evaluations		
	Begin	**Review**	**End**
1. Timothy Johns, the discharge nurse, will go with the Griffins to the pulmonary clinic once a week to help them learn how to use and maintain Ben's oxygen equipment and apnea monitor, including recognizing danger signs.	6/12/90	7/12/90	#7 7/1/90
2. Before Ben is discharged, the Griffins will demonstrate to Timothy their ability to use and maintain Ben's equipment.	6/12/90	7/12/90	7/12/90
3. Timothy will make a list of local vendors and service companies for Ben's medical equipment. Michael will contact these companies and arrange for Ben's needs.	6/15/90	7/8/90	#7 6/22/90
4. Michael will take Ben to the pulmonary clinic once a month to have his levels monitored.	After discharge		

Child's Name: Benjamin Griffin

Date: 6/7/90

Service/Action	Dates and Evaluations		
	Begin	**Review**	**End**
5. Pat White, the Griffin's pediatrician and case coordinator, will visit the Griffin's home to help Leslie teach her friend, Heather, Ben's care procedures. Timothy will look for resource materials to help.	2 weeks before discharge	8/15/90	#7 8/30/90

Criteria/Timeline:

The Griffins will determine if their expressed need has been met, in consultation with Timothy Johns, the discharge nurse.

Child's Name: Benjamin Griffin

Date: 6/7/90

Outcome # 3:

Benjamin needs to develop better feeding skills and increase his motor development.

Identified By: Adrienne Wales, OTR, and supported by Leslie and Michael.

Family Concerns, Priorities, and Resources for This Outcome:

I have the time and a car to drive to the hospital to meet with the therapist before Ben comes home, and to take Ben to weekly sessions with the therapist after he does. I want to learn techniques to use at home, and I want someone to come regularly to our house to be sure all is going well. I'd like these visits to be scheduled when I can arrange for someone to take care of our daughter Caroline. (Leslie)

Service/Action		Dates and Evaluations		
		Begin	Review	End
1.	Adrienne will visit Ben twice a week during the next four weeks to evaluate and monitor his fine motor development and feeding skills.	6/8/90	7/8/90	#7 7/8/90
2.	Adrienne and Ben's primary nurse will show Leslie and Michael how to feed Ben and will help them hold and feed Ben during each visit to the nursery.	6/15/90	7/8/90	#7 7/1/90
3.	Adrienne will begin therapy with Ben as soon as he is medically able.	Open		#7 7/1/90
4.	Adrienne will work with the neonatologist and Dr. White to develop a feeding program for Ben to help him develop a smooth, coordinated suck and swallow.	6/15/90	7/15/90	#7 7/15/90
5.	After discharge, Leslie will bring Ben to the hospital every Tuesday for occupational therapy.	After Discharge	Four weeks after initiation	#7 10/9/90

Child's Name: Benjamin Griffin

Date: 6/7/90

Service/Action	Dates and Evaluations		
	Begin	Review	End
6. During these weekly sessions, Adrienne will show Leslie how to help Ben learn how to use his hands bilaterally and to increase his hand to mouth play.	After discharge	10/1/90	#7 10/9/90
7. Amanda Grey, the infant specialist in the Griffin's community early intervention program, will visit Leslie and Ben once a week to help Leslie carry out Ben's OT activities at home.	After discharge	10/1/90	#5 10/9/90

Criteria/Timeline:

Each activity will begin as specified. Leslie will determine if she is satisfied with Ben's therapy and with the early intervention home visits. Adrienne will monitor Ben's progress by continual clinical observations and through a formal re-assessment using a standarized measure three months after therapy begins.

Child's Name: Benjamin Griffin
Date: 6/7/90

Outcome # 4:

Benjamin needs better feeding skills and he needs to improve his motor development.

Identified By: Kylie Talbot, LPT, and supported by Michael and Leslie.

Family Concerns, Priorities, and Resources for This Outcome:

I have the time and a car to drive to the hospital to meet with the therapist before Ben comes home, and to take Ben to weekly sessions with the therapist after he does. I want to learn techniques to use at home, and I want someone to come to our house regularly, to be sure all is going well. I'd like these visits to be scheduled when I can arrange for someone to take care of our daughter Caroline. (Leslie)

Service/Action		Dates and Evaluations		
		Begin	**Review**	**End**
1.	Kylie will visit Ben twice a week during the next four weeks to evaluate and monitor his gross motor development.	6/8/90	7/8/90	#7 7/8/90
2.	Kylie will begin therapy with Ben as soon as he is medically able.	Open		#7 7/14/90
3.	After discharge, Leslie will bring Ben to the hospital every Tuesday for physical therapy with Kylie.	After discharge	Four weeeks after discharge	#5 10/9/90
4.	Amanda, the infant specialist from the Griffin's community early intervention program, will come to the session with Leslie and Ben once every month to watch Kylie demonstrate the things she wants Leslie to do at home.	After discharge	10/1/90	#5 10/9/90
5.	Leslie will carry out Ben's physical therapy activities at home as shown by Kylie.	After discharge	10/1/90	#5 10/9/90

Child's Name: Benjamin Griffin
Date: 6/7/90

Service/Action	Dates and Evaluations		
	Begin	Review	End
6. During her weekly home visit after Ben's discharge, Amanda will monitor Leslie's use of the techniques Kylie has shown Leslie.	After discharge	10/1/90	#5 10/9/90

Criteria/Timeline:

The activities will be implemented as specified above. Leslie will determine her satisfaction with Ben's therapy. Kylie will monitor Ben's progress by continous clinical observations and through formal re-assessment using a standarized measure every four months.

Child's Name: Benjamin Griffin
Date: 10/9/90

Outcome # **Revision of Outcomes #3-4:**

Outcomes stay the same, but activities and strategies are changing.

Identified By: Leslie

Family Concerns, Priorities, and Resources for This Outcome:

After Ben was discharged and I was responsible for most of his care, my needs have definitely changed. I don't want to spend my time and energy making two separate trips each week to the hospital. Instead, I want to spend more time with Caroline. I'd like Amanda to take over Ben's therapy activities once a week, so I need another visit from Amanda each week. (Leslie)

I now feel more comfortable handling Ben. I also have more time now to take over some of Ben's care from Leslie, including working on therapy. (Michael)

Service/Action	Dates and Evaluations		
	Begin	Review	End
1. Adrienne and Kylie will work together on Ben's OT and PT. They will see Ben together once a week for four weeks, then they will alternate, each seeing Ben every other week.	10/14/90	12/15/90	
2. Adrienne and Kylie have developed the following therapy goals jointly: a. Ben will tolerate a prone position for play for 10 minutes, while supporting himself with his arms and manipulating a toy. b. Ben will manipulate a toy using both hands at midline. c. During feeding, Ben will sit erect, supported, with his head at midline and his chin tucked.	10/14/90	12/15/90	

Child's Name: Benjamin Griffin

Date: 10/9/90

Service/Action	Dates and Evaluations		
	Begin	Review	End
3. Leslie will continue to carry out Ben's program at home, but Michael will now do weekends, and Amanda will visit an extra day each week to be in charge one day.	10/14/90	12/15/90	

Criteria/Timeline:

Ben's progress on the OT/PT joint goals will be clinically evaluated jointly by Adrienne and Kylie. Leslie will decide in eight weeks if she feels the new system is working for her.

Evaluation Rating Scale*

Ratings	Criteria
1	Situation changed or worsened; No longer a need, goal, or project
2	Situation unchanged; Still a need, goal, or project
3	Implementation begun; Still a need, goal, or project
4	Outcome partially attained or accomplished
5	Outcome accomplished or attained, but not to the family's satisfaction
6	Outcome mostly accomplished or attained to the family's satisfaction
7	Outcome completely accomplished or attained to the family's satisfaction

*Source: Deal, A.G., Dunst, C.J., Trivette, C.M. (1989). A flexible and functional approach to the Individualized Family Support Plan. *Infants and Young Children, 1*(4).

Child's Name: Benjamin Griffin
Date: 10/9/90

DATE	NOTES/COMMENTS
6/7/90	The Griffin's IFSP is being developed by an interagency team consisting of the Griffins, their hospital team, the infant specialist from their local early intervention program, and their pediatrician, who will serve as their care coordinator. Benjamin has been making steady progress, and tentative plans are being made to discharge him home in four weeks. This IFSP is being written as his discharge plan.
10/9/90	Leslie and Michael are unhappy with some aspects of their IFSP, and Dr. White has asked the other members of the IFSP team to met with the Griffins and her to make some revisions. Outcomes 3-4, which relate to OT and PT for Benjamin, have been very problematic for Lesile. Having two separate appointments each week on different days means four hours of commuting to the hospital. Leslie is beginning to hate the drive and dislikes leaving Caroline with her neighbor so often. The team discussed options to eliminate this problem. Kylie and Adrienne have agreed to work together in the future, thereby requiring only one visit a week. To meet hospital review board requirements, OT and PT outcomes will be written separately, but therapy will be provided jointly. Initially, Adrienne and Kylie will see Ben together. After they have had a chance to learn each others' activities with Ben, they will alternate, each seeing Ben every other week. Leslie also feels swamped by the demands of carrying out Ben's therapy at home, given all the time she must spend caring for him. She would like some time to spend with Caroline or spend alone and has asked that Amanda come to the house twice a week rather than once a week. Amanda will take over Ben's home therapy during that extra day. Leslie has decided that she now wants to be co-care coordinator with Pat White.

Sample Individualized Family Service Plan #3

The Lain Family

(See vignette #3, Chapter Three, page 27)

The IFSP for the Lain family was written by Adrienne Frank and Corinne Garland of Project Trans/Team at Child Development Resources (CDR) in Lightfoot, Virginia, and Deana Buck, formerly with CDR and now at the Virginia Department of Mental Health/Mental Retardation and Substance Abuse. A committee of parents was formed to develop and evaluate, in collaboration with staff, a family-centered IFSP process to be used by the CDR Infant/Family Program. The committee worked with staff to ensure that both the IFSP process and format enable family members to choose how much of their family life they want to share with the other members of the IFSP team.

The sample IFSP for the Lains is constructed so that a family can decide which parts of the IFSP it wants to share with professionals outside the program -- any section of the IFSP can be easily detached from the other sections before the IFSP is copied and sent elsewhere. On the recommendation of the CDR Parent IFSP Committee, outcomes that primarily concern the child are separated from outcomes that primarily concern the family, further facilitating a family's ability to keep family information private, if it so chooses.

Child Development Resources
Post Office Box 299
Lightfoot, VA 23090
(804) 565-03031

Individualized Family Service Plan

Name: Jennifer Owles
Date of Birth: May 15, 1988
Sex: Female
SSN: 000-00-0000

Legal Guardian: Matt and Olivia Lain
Address: 125 Mory Lane
Phone: 529-0631

Service Coordinator(s): Olivia Lain and James Crane

Assessment Date: 4/25/90

Pertinent History

This is Jennifer's fourth assessment. She was initially assessed at Child Development Resources (CDR) on October 3, 1988, and enrolled in the Infant/Parent Program. At that time, she demonstrated significant delays in all areas of development. Her general lethargic state and frequent seizures were of great concern.

Jennifer's care requires frequent medical appointments and participation in early intervention activities. Since September, Jennifer and Ms. Lain have participated in weekly home visits with Julia Smith, who is both the primary service provider and co-service coordinator with Ms. Lain. Jennifer and Ms. Lain participate in other program activities as her schedule allows. She has occasionally attended parent group meetings while Jennifer has participated in center based activities. A representative of the Virginia Commission for the Visually Handicapped observed Jennifer at CDR in January and gave Ms. Lain several activities to try at home. On September 10th, Jennifer was seen at CDR by Dr. Lock, pediatric neurologist.

Jennifer's daily care has consisted of handling and positioning, chest physical therapy, and special feeding procedures. Since Ms. Lain has assumed responsibility for Jennifer's care, and since a change in medication, significant developmental gain has been made and Jennifer has been in good health. Her tolerance for being handled is still very low, although she is now able to calm herself after having been upset.

Ms. Lain gradually assumed, with the consent of Jennifer's mother, primary responsibility for Jennifer's care. Jenny has lived with Ms. Lain since she was six months old. Ms. Lain initiated a recommendation for a change in medication that resulted in significantly diminished seizure activity and considerably longer periods of alertness and responsiveness. Although she is delighted with Jennifer's new alertness, responsiveness, and developmental progress, Ms. Lain states that she is fearful that if Jennifer makes too much progress, Jenny's mother will change her mind about giving up custody. Ms. Lain is quite attached to Jenny now and would like to plan for her life as part of the Lain family.

Referral

Source: Children's Hospital referral through Hometown Health Department
Reason for Referral: History of seizures
Date: 8/25/88

Medical or Developmental Evaluations

Type of Information	Agency or Individual	Date Received
Birth history	Lightfoot Community Hospital	10/1/88
Pediatric Care	Dr. Toi, Health Department	9/18/88
Medical Care	Children's Hospital	10/9/88
	Neurology Clinic	4/14/89
		10/6/89
		3/21/90

Service Providers

Role	Agency	Address & Phone	Contact Person
Referral source	Health Department	20 First St. 244-2300	Mrs. Watson
Dr. Toi (primary physician)	Health Department	20 First St. 244-2300	
Comprehensive early intervention services	Infant/Parent Program	(see above)	Ellen Porter
	JCC Social Services	21 First St. 353-5443	Cathy Smith
Neurology Center	Children's Hospital	Big City, VA 229-0012	Lauren Gray

Part I. Child Assessment

Assessment Team Members:

Olivia Lain, Guardian, Co-Service Coordinator
Mary Larson, Physical Therapist (Assessment Facilitator)
Barbara Rupp, Speech Pathologist
Ann Olsen, Educator
James Crane, Primary Service Provider and Co-Case Manager

Special Considerations for Assessment:

Jennifer is anxious around strangers, and her primary service provider suggested that only one team member handle her during assessment. The physical therapist was chosen because of Jennifer's history of poor quality movement. Dr. Toi, pediatrician, and Dr. Lock, pediatric neurologist, were unable to attend the assessment. Their input was provided during telephone conferences with the service coordinator and has been noted in the assessment report.

Assessment Instruments Used:

Jennifer was assessed using a transdisciplinary arena process in which all team members made observations in all areas of development. Portions of the following assessment instruments were used to guide the clinical observations of the team:

Early Learning Accomplishment Profile (E-LAP)
Receptive-Expressive Emergent Language Scale (REEL)
Infant Scale of Communicative Intent (ISCI)
Uzgiris-Hunt Scales of Infant Development (U-H)
Social-Emotional Development Profile (SEED)
Hawaii Early Learning Profile (HELP)

Child Assessment -- Strengths, Concerns, and Development Levels:

Strengths

Jennifer has made a great deal of progress since her last assessment. Dr. Lock, pediatric neurologist, confirmed that her seizure activity has decreased, which has allowed her to enjoy playing with toys and interacting with new people. Overall, there has been a significant change in the way Jenny moves and in the way in which she uses her muscles. Her interest in interacting with family members and strangers has increased, as has her participation in new experiences (toys, games, and textures). She has also improved in her use of eyes and hands together.

During the assessment, Jenny used several new skills, including sitting independently for a few seconds when placed. While sitting, she was able to look around at the items in the room, although she was unable to manipulate objects in that position. She made eye contact with Olivia, her foster mother, and with several of the assessment team members.

There has been much improvement in the quality of Jennifer's movement. She got up onto her hands and knees several times. Although she did not crawl during the assessment, it seemed as if she was getting ready to do so. She spent a great deal of the time during the assessment on her stomach, and was able to track items a full 180 degrees from that position. As she visually followed an object, she turned her head and rolled from stomach to back and back to stomach. She was able to track the object horizontally and vertically.

Jenny enjoyed several activities during the assessment and smiled when favorite toys were presented. She seemed to remember where certain toys were placed and tried to move toward them. Playing with toys she could hold was fun for Jennifer, although she had a hard time maintaining a firm grasp on objects. She did pass a block from one hand to the other. She put objects into her mouth using both hands. She put both hands in a container to retrieve an object. She also used her body to trap an object. Jennifer enjoyed playing some games and initiated some with Olivia, who reported that Jenny likes to play "Peek-a-boo" and "Pat-a-cake" at home.

Jenny communicated in many different ways using smiles, eye contact, and sounds. She made several sounds during the assessment, including many vowels "ah," "oh," "a," and "uh," and a few consonants, "g," "k," which are sounds made in the back of the throat. She seems to understand many words, looking at an item discussed and responding to a request when paired with a gesture. When Olivia asked her for a kiss, Jenny moved toward her and attempted a kiss. Olivia said Jennifer knows the names of many common objects in the house and that she knows what many food words mean. When hungry, Jenny communicates her need by smacking her lips together and by moving her mouth and lips. When she drinks from a bottle, she places both hands on the bottle but does not hold it. She tries to grasp the spoon while being fed.

Since the change in her medication, the quality of Jenny's movements is much improved, and her level of alertness is greatly improved. She enjoys making a variety of sounds, and she uses them as a way of showing her happiness as well as her frustration. She calms to the sound of Olivia's voice or with physical contact (hugs and kisses). Jenny has a brief attention span during which she likes to play games with family members.

Concerns

Jennifer's development seems to be influenced by problems with vision and by low muscle tone. Jenny's eyes wandered during the assessment, and her left eye had small horizontal movements (nystagmus). Olivia said she had noticed the same thing at home and that Jennifer's vision is monitored by the ophthalmologists at Children's Hospital. Jennifer's eye movements make it difficult for her to focus on small items, to line items up, or to put items together. Judging distances (depth perception) will improve as she continues to use her eyes together.

Currently, Jenny enjoys being on her stomach on the floor. Her reduced strength in her head and upper body (trunk) affect her movement in and out of sitting. Using her arms to prop herself in sitting interferes with Jennifer's ability to play with objects using both hands. Even when supported in sitting, Jenny can't maintain a firm grasp on objects and has a difficult time controlling her movements. As her back and front muscles get stronger, Jennifer will develop the trunk strength she will need for crawling and walking.

Jennifer's reduced trunk strength also affects her ability to control air flow for speech. As Jenny played, her mouth was almost always open. This prevented her from making many sounds like "b," "p," or "m," which require lip closure. Although Jenny used many vowel sounds during the assessment and used them to communicate a great deal of information, she used few consonant sounds. Jenny used no gestures during assessment, and the only gesture that Olivia has observed is Jenny smacking or moving her lips when she wants to eat. Jennifer has a short attention span and was not interested in looking at books or in other activities that required her attention for more than a few seconds.

Jennifer's delays in cognitive development, particularly her ability to imitate, are also related to her lack of mobility. As her motor development improves, she will be able to participate more in turn-taking activities, give and take games, and games where her action causes a reaction (cause/effect games). As Jenny continues to be interested in what's going on around her and is able to move about to explore, she will learn more about objects and how they are used.

Summary of Developmental Levels Based on Assessment

The summary of developmental levels is only useful in the context of the proceeding discussion of development and should not be used separately.

Gross Motor	4-8 months
Fine Motor	6-7 months
Receptive Language	7-8 months
Expressive Language	6-7 months
Cognitive	6-9 months
Social	6-8 months
Self-Help	5-6 months

PART II. Family Concerns, Priorities, and Resources

Olivia identified the following strengths and concerns during weekly home visits with the primary service provider, during Jenny's assessment, and during the IFSP planning meeting.

Strengths and Resources:

Olivia's daily care of Jennifer has resulted in significant improvement in Jennifer's health and development. Olivia says that her work schedule is flexible enough to allow her to keep Jennifer's doctor's appointments and that she is interested in remaining involved in Jennifer's early intervention program when her schedule allows.

Olivia says that her husband, Matt, says he likes to play with Jennifer and is more willing to take care of her while Olivia is at work now that her seizures are controlled and she is more interesting to be with. Olivia's friend, Bea, expressed interest in baby-sitting and having an occasional home visit from the early intervention program for help in learning some new activities for Jennifer.

Concerns:

Olivia wants Jennifer to use words and have new ways to play with toys. She wants her to learn to walk. She is less concerned, however, with Jenny's motor development than with feeding and speech because she is so encouraged by Jenny's gains in sitting and belly crawling. She also wants information about starting Jenny on some new foods.

Olivia is concerned about her heavy work schedule and how she can continue to participate in the infant program home visits, especially given Jenny's many medical care appointments. She has expressed a concern for how, given her difficult schedule, she can meet Jenny's complex developmental needs. She has some toys at home for Jenny, but wants help in finding new ways to use them. She also wants some respite from child care. Right now all her time is spent at work or caring for Jenny. Olivia knows that Jenny may be eligible for the program for preschool children with handicaps in the fall and has expressed an interest in learning more about that program.

Olivia is also interested in involving Jennifer's mother in the early intervention program. She is also concerned about custody issues and how to go about legally adopting Jennifer.

PART III. Outcomes Related to Child Development

Full team review at next team assessment (projected date 7/15/90). Ongoing review to be conducted by parent, service coordinator, and assessment team members.

---

1. OUTCOME: Jennifer will increase her oral motor skills in order to eat more easily and to be able to make more sounds.

A. Objective: Jennifer will eat several new thick textured foods.

Strategies:

1. Olivia will check with Dr. Toi about offering Jennifer more table foods.
2. One new thick textured food will be offered each week (mashed potatoes, lumpy bananas, chunky apple sauce, crackers).
3. Early Learning Activities (ELA) Self-Help 4: Eating thick textured foods.

Person(s) Responsible: Parent, pediatrician

Criteria: As specified in the strategies above, observation/report by team member(s)

Review/ Modify: 6/90, or before as needed

Status:

B. Objective: Jennifer will frequently combine "b," "m," and "p" sounds with vowel sounds in babbling.

Strategies:

1. Pairing sounds with toys in play and during feeding.
   Hawaii Early Learning Profile (HELP) 2.22

Person(s) Responsible: Parent, primary service provider, day care teacher

Criteria: As specified in the strategies above, observation/report by team member(s)

Review/ Modify: 7/15/90, or before as needed

Status:

C. Objective: Jennifer will imitate a variety of consonant and vowel combinations in turn-taking games with adults. (Combinations such as "ah-good," "da-da," "ma-ma").

Strategies:
1. Learning Through Play (LTP): p. 142, Task B.
2. LTP: p. 168, Task D

Person(s) Responsible: Parent, primary service provider, day care teacher

Criteria: As specified in the strategies above, observation/report by team member(s)

Review/ Modify: 7/15/90, or before as needed

Status:

D. Objective: Jennifer will drink from cup, keeping her lips closed and losing only small amounts of liquid.

Strategies:
1. Cup drinking at meals and snacks, assisting with jaw support as needed. Olivia will be given a variety of cups to try with Jennifer.

2. ELA Self-Help 6: Provide jaw support from front
3. ELA Self-Help 7: Provide jaw support from side

Person(s) Responsible: Parent, primary service provider, day care teacher

Criteria: As specified in the strategies above, observation/report by team member(s)

Review/ modify: 7/15/90, or before as needed

Status:

---

2. OUTCOME: Jennifer will improve her understanding of language in order to communicate with her family and playmates.

A. Objective: Jennifer will sit with an adult to look at a story book for 1-2 minutes daily while objects are named and actions are discussed.

Strategies:
1. ELA Language 36: Look at and point to pictures in book.
2. ELA Language 37: Use homemade books with pictures of familiar objects

Person(s) Responsible: Parent, primary service provider, day care teacher

Criteria: As specified in the strategies above, observation/report by team member(s)

Review/ modify: 6/15/90, or before as needed

Status:

B. Objective: Jennifer will frequently follow one-step directions such as "get the ball," "give me the bear."

Strategies:

1. ELA Language 23: Responding to verbal request, e.g., up, give me, etc.
2. ELA Language 24: Responding to simple requests without hints.

Person(s) Responsible: Parent, primary service provider, day care teacher

Criteria: As specified in the strategies above, observation/report by team member(s)

Review/ modify: 7/15/90, or before as needed

Status:

---

3. OUTCOME: Jennifer will improve her balance and strength in the muscles of her trunk to enable her to sit independently for playing and to prepare her for later crawling and walking.

A. Objective: Jennifer will improve her head and trunk control in order to sit unsupported.

Strategies:

1. Home Program Instruction Sheets for Infants and Young Children (Yaeger) C-1: Pulling to sit supported by adult's hands around upper arms and shoulders.
2. Yaeger C-19: Sitting and reaching (adapted by sitting Jennifer on floor between adult's legs).
3. Yaeger C-3: Moves from prone to sitting.
4. Yaeger C-5: Moves from hands to knees to sitting.
5. Rocking to music on hands and knees.
6. Continuing consultation with physical therapist.

Person(s) Responsible: Parent, primary service provider

Criteria: As specified in the strategies above, observation/report by team member(s)

Review/ modify: 7/15/90, or before as needed

Status:

B. Objective: Jennifer will sit without support, using two hands to play.

Strategies: These activities may be started in side lying or supported sitting while Jennifer is learning to sit independently.

1. Play movement games like "row, row, row your boat" and other nursery rhymes while sitting.
2. Yaeger S-9: Tilting on lap.
3. Yaeger S-10: Lateral tilt (sitting on legs).
4. ELA Gross Motor 38: Uses muscles of all sides of trunk to remain sitting.
5. ELA Gross Motor 39: Grasps object while supported in sitting.
6. ELA Gross Motor 53: Bears weight on arms while sitting.

Person(s) Responsible: Parent, primary service provider, day care teacher

Criteria: As specified in the strategies above, observation/report by team member(s)

Review/ modify: 7/15/90, or before as needed

Status:

---

4. OUTCOME: Jennifer will improve her ability to use her eyes and hands together so that she will have a variety of ways to play with toys alone and with her family.

A. Objective: Jennifer will imitate at least three hand motions in play or for social games.

Strategies:

1. LTP p. 216: Imitating new gestures.
2. ELA Social 12-18: Social imitation games -- Wave bye bye, clap hands, point to object in play, push car, roll ball, pat doll, bang with hammer, cup filling and dumping.

Person(s)
Responsible: Parent, primary service provider, day care teacher

Criteria: As specified in the strategies above, observation/report by team member(s)

Review/
modify: 7/15/90, or before as needed

Status:

B. Objective: Jennifer will play with toys using both hands.

Strategies:

1. Any play involving use of two objects together -- blocks, small balls, small cars or people, toys with attached parts (school bus, etc.)

2. Work with Olivia to find toys and objects at home that can be used in play. Lend toys from library or CDR (Adapt toys as needed).

3. LTP p. 155: Exploring objects with fingers.

4. LTP p. 156: Combining two objects in functional manner.

5. LTP p. 157: Using hands to manipulate several objects.

6. ELA Fine Motor 9: Holds toy with two hands.

7. ELA Fine Motor 12: Pulls out large peg from pegboard.

Person(s)
Responsible: Parent, primary service provider, day care teacher

Criteria: As specified in the strategies above, observation/report by team member(s)

Review/
modify: 7/15/90, or before as needed

Status:

Part IV: Other Outcomes Desired By The Family

---

1. OUTCOME: Olivia will have ways to plan for Jennifer's future custody.

Objective: Access agencies or professionals in the community who can help Olivia plan for Jennifer's future.

Strategies:

1. Provide Olivia with assistance, as needed, in scheduling meetings with Jennifer's case worker.
2. Request meeting with Barbara, case worker, and service coordinator to plan for Jennifer's future and to determine Barbara's present and future role.
3. Provide names and phone numbers of other resources: Legal Aid, Agency of Adoption, etc.

Person(s) Responsible: Parent, co-service coordinator

Criteria: As specified in the strategies above, observation/report by team member(s)

Review: 5/30/90 (in 2 months)

Status:

---

2. OUTCOME: The family will be provided with information about available respite resources in the community.

Objective: To explore and locate respite options.

Strategies:

1. Explore family and neighborhood options for child care.
2. Provide information about local respite care program.
3. CDR to provide center-based care opportunity.

Person(s) Responsible: Parent, co-service coordinator

Criteria: Parent satisfaction with information provided

Review: 5/30/90 (in 6 weeks)

Status:

3. OUTCOME: **Jennifer's home program will be adapted in order to involve Barbara to the level and extent she desires.**

Objective: Determine Barbara's interest in program and adapt program as needed.

Strategies:

1. The service coordinator will request a meeting with Barbara to discuss her interest in participating in early intervention activities.
2. The team will make adaptations in the plan as determined by Barbara, with Olivia's consent and approval.
3. The service coordinator will meet with Barbara, as negotiated.
4. The service coordinator will offer Barbara home visits in a neutral setting (e.g., church, community center).

Person(s) Responsible: Parent, co-service coordinator

Criteria: By parent report, co-service coordinator observation/notes

Review: 6/90 (in 3 months)

Status:

PART V: Early Intervention Program Services

1. Twice monthly home visits by James Crane, primary service provider, and co-service coordinator, to be scheduled for late afternoon, after Olivia returns from work. One visit each month by James with babysitter, Bea.

2. An integrated center-based play group is available for Jennifer on Tuesday and Wednesday mornings to be used as frequently as Olivia chooses. The person responsible for the program is Eula May Barlow.

3. Parent group meetings are available once a week on Tuesday or Wednesday as Olivia's and Matt's schedules allow. Kathleen Phillips is the staff representative to the parent group meeting.

4. Dr. Lock, pediatric neurology consultant to the early intervention program, is available for neurological consultation with the team as needed. Dr. Toi, pediatrician, will provide continuing health care supervision.

5. Continue consultation with Virginia Commission for the Visually Impaired when possible (at least once per year, more frequently as needed).

6. Olivia and James Crane will explore options for transition, including a visit to the Preschool Center later in the spring. They will use the CDR transition notebook to help them develop a transition plan. Transition will be the topic for parent group meetings during the next two months and Olivia will see if she can adapt her schedule to attend the meetings.

Projected Dates and Duration

Immediate implementation of plan (home visit, June 12, 1990). To continue until formal reassessment in six months (December 1990), unless revised prior to this date.

IFSP Record

IFSP	Review Date	Project Duration
10/3/88	December	1/13/89
1/13/89	March	6/10/89
3/12/89	June	9/18/89
9/25/90	January	3/13/91

IFSP Team

Family:

I had the opportunity to participate in the development of this IFSP. I understand the plan, and I give permission to the Infant/Parent Program to carry out the plan with me, leading toward the agreed upon outcomes.

Olivia Lain Matt Lain 4/25/90

Parent(s)/Legal Guardian(s) Date

I had the opportunity to participate in the development of this IFSP. I do not agree with this plan and I do not give my permission to the Infant-Program to carry out the plan.

Parent(s)/Legal Guardian(s) Date

Other IFSP Meeting Participants:

The following individuals participated in the development of the IFSP. Each person understands and agrees to carry out the plan as it applies to their role in the provision of services.

Olivia Lain

Olivia Lain
Legal Guardian

Barbara Rupp

Barbara Rupp, MA, CCC-SP
Infant-Parent Program

James Crane

James Crane
Primary Service Provider/Co-Service Coordinator

Mary Larson, R.P.T.

Mary Larson, R.P.T.
Infant-Parent Program

Ann Olsen, M.Ed.

Ann Olsen, M.ED.
Infant-Parent Program

Bryan Taylor, M.S.W.

Bryan Taylor, M.S.W.
Hometown Social Services
Child and Family Services

The IFSP was developed with telephone consultation from the following people:
Dr. Toi, Pediatrician
Dr. Lock, Pediatric Neurologist

Sample Individualized Family Service Plan #4

The Mack Family

(See vignette #4, Chapter Three, pages 27-28)

The IFSP for the Mack family was written by Mary Ann Sampon, Jeanette Myers, and Andrea Alder at Project LIFT of the Portage Projects in Portage, Wisconsin, and George Jesien, now at the University of Wisconsin-Madison. These IFSP developers submitted a comprehensive IFSP record for the Mack family, covering the period from referral to Project LIFT to transition into a public school early childhood program. This IFSP included many revisions that demonstrated how child and family concerns, priorities, and resources change over time and carefully chosen clinical strategies and activities. The IFSP that appears in this document, however, was considerably shortened because of page limitations -- only parts of the first and last IFSP for the Mack family were included. The editors chose this approach so that both the Developmental Record and Transition Plan and Record developed by Project LIFT could be included as models for the IFSP process.

Date of Referral: March 1, 1989
Beginning IFSP Date: 3/89
Review Dates: 9/89, 4/90, 9/90

Project LIFT
INDIVIDUALIZED FAMILY SERVICE PLAN

Child's Name: Lita Mack
Date of Birth: October 2, 1988
Current Placement/Services: Project LIFT
Mother's Name: Dee
Phone (home): 528-5999
Father's Name: Mark
Phone (home): 528-5999
Care Coordinator: Pauline Carter

County of Residence: Columbia
School District: Lodi

Address: 1422 Brown Street
(work): 529-0371
Address: 1422 Brown Street
(work): 729-0631
Phone: LIFT

EEN/Diagnosis: Prematurity -- Bronchopulmonary Dysplasia -- off oxygen in May, 1990.

Medical Information

Vision: Amblyopia
Hearing: Within normal limits.
Medication: Bactrim, Chlorothyroide, Aldactone
Precautions: Frequent vomiting following oral or G-tube feedings of more than 4 ounces.

IFSP Committee

IFSP Committee		Date
Parent(s):	Mark Mack	3/17/89
	Dee Mack	3/17/89
Teacher:	Nancy [illegible]	3/17/89
Therapist:	George Cashel	3/17/89
County Representative:	Gena June	3/17/89
LEA Representative:		

		Date
Nurse/Pediatrician:	Josiana Wistman	3/17/89
Social Worker:	Pamela Card	3/17/89
Advocate:		
Other:		

Project LIFT

DEVELOPMENTAL HISTORY

Date: February, 1989
Child's Name: Lita **DOB:** October 2, 1988
Address: 1422 Brown Street
Phone: 608-528-5999

FAMILY COMPOSITION

Mother: Dee, age 27, optometric assistant
Father: Mark, age 37, carpenter
Step Parent:
Foster Parent:
Other Children:

Name	Age
Jeremy	2

How are other child(ren) feeling towards Lita?

Okay -- sometimes Jeremy is too active around Lita.

Others Living in Home:

None

Do you have family and friends close by that help and spend time with the children?

Grandparents, Relatives:

My sister was very helpful when Lita was first born, but our family tends to shy away from Lita right now -- they think she's too fragile.

PREGNANCY

Pregnancy was ____ **normal** _X_ **problems**
If problems, what kind: (please circle)

chronic disease **viral infection** **Rh incompatibility**
vaginal bleeding **toxemia** **hypertension** **trauma**
other: 4 months spotting -- heavier bleeding

BIRTH HISTORY

Child's weight: 1 lb., 9 1/2 oz.
Length of labor: ____________________
Special considerations: (please circle)

cesarian	**cord around neck**
premature (# of weeks): 28	**jaundiced**
breech	**transfused**
baby rotated	**twin (1st born, 2nd born)**
Rh negative	**other**____________________

Born at 28 weeks gestational age

Length of child's hospital stay: Lita was in incubator 2 1/2 months

What was it like for you while your child was in the hospital?

We were very worried. We didn't know if she would make it or whether she might be permanently disabled.

List any special cares that were needed (such as oxygen, incubator, tube feedings, surgery):

Incubator
Oxygen
Tube feedings

Now that your child is out of the hospital, how are you feeling about caring for him/her at home? About being a parent?

I feel confident in caring for her. I want to treat her like any other baby.

EARLY LIFE

Tell me about your child when he/she was an infant? (How he/she first came home from the hospital.)

As a newborn my child was:

Very small and fragile. Lita needed oxygen and lots of care. She was very, very quiet. She slept 14 hours.

Does she/he have any developed routines for sleeping?

Sleep habits: Lita sleeps 14 hours then wakes for feeding. She's awake 2 or 3 hours at a time.

slept well **slept restlessly** **hardly slept** **never napped**

Tell me about meal times for your child, is it pleasant or a difficult time?

Feeding habits: Lita eats 6 times a day. (70 cc per feeding - G-tube Similac.) She will try a 4 oz. bottle with flexible nipple.

ate well **difficulty sucking** **difficulty swallowing**

food allergies **other:** The 4 a.m. feeding can be difficult -- she wants to sleep.

How do/did you feel during these first months?

We are happy to have her home. We're sometimes tired by night feedings, but we feel generally good.

MEDICAL HISTORY

Are there ongoing health concerns?

Yes. Lita is currently on oxygen and has an apnea monitor. She has a cardiac murmur and had severe bronchopulmonary dysplasia. Lita has severe vomiting following oral or G-tube feeding -- cause unknown.

Has your child had:

Any major illnesses? Yes

Any hospitalizations?
1. Cardiac surgery -- valve set -- heart and lungs
2. G-I virus
3. Vomiting and weight loss

Are there any special things you've noticed that seem unusual or that concern you about your child?

History of ear infections? None **If yes, how many?**

Is your child receiving any medications? yes ___ **no** _X_

If yes, please list:

Lacix
Symopholin
Aldactone

HEARING

How does your child respond to sounds? Does he like or dislike certain sounds or voices, or types of music?

Lita loves music and people talking to her.

Do you feel your child has difficulty hearing? yes ___ **no** _X_

If yes, are there certain situations where he/she responds better to auditory stimuli?

Has your child ever had a formal hearing evaluation?

yes ___ **no** _X_

Where:

When:

Results:

VISION

Are there any special things you've noticed about your child's response to light or the way he/she uses his/her eyes and vision?

Seems fine.

Do you feel your child has any visual difficulties?

yes __X__ **no** ____
Please describe: far-sighted -- no major concerns

Has he/she received a formal vision evaluation?

yes __X__ **no** ____
Where: Davis & Dueur
When: February, 1989
Results: far-sighted -- amblyopia -- mild

DEVELOPMENTAL MILESTONES

Tell me some of the things your baby can do.

Too little -- she mostly sleeps.

At what age did your child first: N/A -- too young. C.A. 4 month adjusted C.A. 1 month

roll __________ **say first word** __________
sit __________ **finger feed** __________
walk __________ **use spoon** __________
drink from cup __________

Do you have special concerns or questions about his/her development?

We have some concerns about weight gain. How do premature babies do over time? Will she be an oral feeder? Vomiting is a major concern right now.

CURRENT HABITS

My child currently:

sleeps/naps:	**inconsistently**	**well**	**restlessly**
eats/drinks:	**at regular intervals** **consistent amounts**	**at inconsistent intervals** **inconsistent amounts**	

Comments: The 4 a.m. feeding is difficult. Lita is starting to vomit after feeding, and we are concerned about this.

HELPING OTHERS KNOW YOUR BABY

What are some of the ways he/she lets you know what he/she wants?

Cries, looks at me, moves around.

How do you know when he/she is happy? sad? scared? mad?

Cries when sad or mad or scared. Quiet when content.

Does he like to be held or rocked?

Yes

What does he/she do when he/she falls or is hurt?

Cries

How does he/she respond to sitter? stranger?

We don't have her with others at this point.

My child gets around the room by: N/A

Please list any physicians, therapists, social workers, or other professionals working with your child.

Name	Agency	Title
K. Smith	Columbia County WIC	Public Health Nurse
Dr. Feinstein	East Madison Clinic	
Dr. Rud	St. Mary's ICC	
Dr. Kenneth	St. Mary's ICC	
Dr. Bradley	St. Mary's Hospital	Pulmonary doctor
Dr. Tuttle	St. Mary's Hospital	Cardiac doctor

Date: 3/89
Updates:

INDIVIDUALIZED FAMILY SERVICE PLAN

Child: Lita Mack **Area:** Motor

Present Level of Functioning	Outcomes (Who, What Help, Degree of Success)	Intervention/ Strategies/Materials	Timelines/Person Responsible		
			Initiation	Changed/ Achieved	Review Date/ Comments
Lita is beginning to gain head control in an upright position at her mother's shoulder.	For Lita to increase her head and trunk control when she is lying on her stomach.	Place Lita over a small 3" wedge for short periods of time (2-3 minutes). Provide less support for short periods of time in different positions.	5/89	10/89	
Lita has equal movement in both arms and legs, but she favors the left side with her head.	For Lita to learn to use both sides of her body.	Encourage head turning to midline by presenting face and toys from right. Place Lita on both sides in side-lying for toy and hand play.	4/89	9/89	
Lita maintains all-fours position for 30-60 seconds.	For Lita to strengthen her shoulders and elbows in preparation for crawling and pushing up into a sitting position.	Put Lita on her forearms several times every day and help her practice pushing up from her stomach and taking weight on her arms.	3/90	8/90	

Date: 3/89

INDIVIDUALIZED FAMILY SERVICE PLAN

Family: Dee - mother, Mark - father, Lita, Jeremy - brother

Present Level of Functioning	Outcomes (Who, What Help, Degree of Success)	Intervention/ Strategies/Materials	Timelines/Person Responsible		
			Initiation	Changed/ Achieved	Review Date/ Comments
Dee and Mark do not know other parents of children with special needs and would like to be matched with other parents.	To link Dee and Mark with other parents of children who have special needs so that they can share ideas, successes, and challenges.	Identify other parents willing to meet regularly with Mark and Dee.	4/1/89		Care Coordinator and other team members
		Share their names and phone numbers with Mark and Dee.	by 4/15/89		Care Coordinator
		Make the initial contact.	4/15/89		Family by 5/1/89
		Check back to see how things are working.	6/1/89		Care Coordinator monthly

Date: 3/89
Review: 3/90

FAMILY INFORMATION

Family Members and Relationship: Dee - mother; Mark - father; Lita; Jeremy - brother

Instrument (if any):	Date Administered:	By Whom:
Family Needs Survey, Bailey and Simeonson, 1985	3/16/89	J. Brinckerhoff
Daily Routine	3/10/89	Dee
Family Needs Survey	3/7/90	Dee

STRENGTHS

The Macks say that they enjoy spending time together and that they work well together as a family. Lita has opportunities to go out with the family. Dee likes to play with Lita, and they respond well to each other. Jeremy interacts with Lita in a loving manner. The Macks' informal supports are positive and diversified.

NEEDS

Jeremy needs a routine that includes a special time for him and his parents. The Macks would like a parent-to-parent match and perhaps a fathers' group for Mark.

Strengths Update

Date: 3/90

Dee applied for both SSI and Katie Beckett assistance and received confirmation in March 1990.

Jefferson Home Health will be providing nursing care for Lita when Dee delivers their third child on 4/25. This service will be paid for by Medical Assistance.

Jeremy presently goes to a certified babysitter twice a week. This service is paid for by the Families Under Stress Program in Columbia County.

Needs Update

Date: 3/90

Dee would like help locating babysitters/respite care for Lita.

Dee would like help paying for a babysitter/respite worker.

Date: 3/89

ASSESSMENT INFORMATION

Child's Name: Lita Mack **DOB:** 10/2/88

Instrument (if any):	Date Administered:	By Whom:
Bayley Scales	1/17/89	K. Wollenburg
Clinical Observations	3/10/89	J. Brinckerhoff
Carolina Curriculum for Handicapped Infants	3/17/89	A. Alder
Assessment Log	5/5/89	J. Brinckerhoff

STRENGTHS	NEEDS
Motor: Despite Lita's rough start, she has symmetrical movements in her arms and legs. For her size, Lita is active. Communication: Lita gives her mother clear signals with her facial expressions and uses her gaze to express likes and dislikes. Social: Lita is comforted easily by her mother. She smiles reciprocally and distinguishes between her mother and others. Auditory: Lita can hear sounds from all directions. Cognition: Lita reaches toward objects and bats them with her hands.	Lita's primary need is to stabilize her health, put on weight, and strengthen her head and trunk control. Feeding: Use a cylindrical bottle and a premature nipple for bottle feedings. Motor: Promote Lita's use of both sides of her body when she moves. Increase functional hand use.

Strengths/Needs Update **Date:** ________

Date: 3/89
Updates:

INDIVIDUALIZED FAMILY SERVICE PLAN

Child: Lita Mack **Area:** Motor (continued)

Present Level of Functioning	Outcomes (Who, What Help, Degree of Success)	Intervention/ Strategies/Materials	Timelines/Person Responsible		
			Initiation	Changed/ Achieved	Review Date/ Comments
Lita is beginning to use her thumb when she grasps objects.	For Lita to learn to pick up and hold toys and other objects with a better grasp.	Use a variety of different-shaped objects that require more refined grasp patterns (fat objects, thin objects, cup with handle).	3/89	8/90 ongoing	
Lita's endurance is poor. She sits with moderate support from an adult.	For Lita to increase her endurance and improve her sitting balance.	Decrease support when Lita is put in a sitting position. Try this often.	3/89	7/90	
Lita sits in an infant seat and walker.	The care coordinator will find other supportive seats for Lita now that she is getting too big for her infant seat.	Contact therapists at St. Mary's.	3/90	6/90	

Date: 3/89
Updates: ____

INDIVIDUALIZED FAMILY SERVICE PLAN

Child: Lita Mack **Area:** Cognition/Communication

Present Level of Functioning	Outcomes (Who, What Help, Degree of Success)	Intervention/ Strategies/Materials	Timelines/Person Responsible		
			Initiation	Changed/ Achieved	Review Date/ Comments
Lita presently imitates some sounds.	For Lita to imitate oral movements and simple sounds.	Model tongue flapping, lipsmacking, puckering, etc. with and without sound in play. Use mirror — have Lita look in mirror as you do oral movements.	12/89	8/90 ongoing	
Lita inconsistently allows oral stimulation.	For Lita to explore objects with her mouth.	Continue to use soft washcloth with pressure on face. Touch objects to lips in play.	12/89	7/90 with hand only	

Date: 9/90 (Review)

ASSESSMENT INFORMATION
Update

Child's Name: Lita Mack **DOB:** 10/2/88

Instrument:	Date Administered:	By Whom:
REEL	9/13/90	J. Myers, SLP
Carolina (review)	9/13/90	A. Alder, OTR
Preschool Language Scale (PLS)	9/13/90	J. Myers, SLP

STRENGTHS	NEEDS

Strengths/Needs Update Date: 9/90

Strengths	Needs
Lita is very social and enjoys interacting with others. She is using many vocalizations (babbling, jargon, true words) and gestures to express her wants and needs. She is showing more appropriate play with objects.	Lita needs a complete feeding assessment to find out why she continues to vomit. Lita needs to continue her development of receptive/expressive language skills and oral motor skills. Lita needs an increased attention span for all activities.

Date: 9/90 (Review)

FAMILY INFORMATION
Update

Family Members and Relationship: Dee - mother; Mark - father; Lita; Jeremy - brother

Instrument (if any):	Date Administered:	By Whom:
Family Needs Survey	10/5/90	Dee

STRENGTHS	NEEDS

Strengths/Needs Update **Date:** 9/90

Strengths	Needs
Both parents are very active in their children's care. Dee is very involved with Lita's care and extremely knowledgeable about Lita's medical needs.	Dee has expressed some concern about Jeremy's uncooperativeness at the babysitters when he is involved in preacademic groups (i.e., identifying colors and counting).

Date: 9/90
Updates:

INDIVIDUALIZED FAMILY SERVICE PLAN

Family: Dee - mother, Mark - father, Lita, Jeremy - brother

Present Level of Functioning	Outcomes (Who, What Help, Degree of Success)	Problem Solving Steps	Timelines/Person Responsible: Initiation	Changed/ Achieved	Review Date/ Comments
Lita is currently receiving 16 hours of home nursing care, but because her health is improving, she will soon be ineligible for home nursing.	To help the family locate and use babysitting and respite care services as needed.	Identify other sources of care for Lita.	10/1/90		Care Coordinator by 10/15/90
		Help the family contact these agencies, if needed.			Family and Care Coordinator (as needed) by 10/30/90
		Dee and Mark choose care providers after interviewing and observing them with Lita.			Family by 11/30/90
		Help the family train new care providers in how to work with Lita.			Care Coordinator and Family by 12/10/90
	Help find financial assistance to pay for these services.	Contact local social service and family support agencies.			Family and Care Coordinator by 12/1/90 Review Date by 12/15/90

Date: 9/90
Updates:

INDIVIDUALIZED FAMILY SERVICE PLAN

Family: Dee - mother, Mark - father, Lita, Jeremy - brother

Present Level of Functioning	Outcomes (Who, What Help, Degree of Success)	Problem Solving Steps	Timelines/Person Responsible		
			Initiation	Changed/ Achieved	Review Date/ Comments
Dee and Mark are concerned about Jeremy's lack of pre-academic skills.	To help the family find way to increase Jeremy's preacademic skills.	Help Dee and Mark identify Jeremy's needs.	9/1/90		Care Coordinator by 9/10/90
		Assess Jeremy for possible referral to 3-5 programs			Family and Care Coordinator by 9/20/90
	To investigate options for preschool Head Start Programs.	Investigate preschool options with Dee and Mark.			Family by 9/30/90
		Dee and Mark choose schools to observe and set up dates.			Family by 10/15/90
		Dee and Mark decide the best option for Jeremy and enroll him in the program.			Review Date 10/20/90

Project LIFT

Date: 9/90
Updates:

INDIVIDUALIZED FAMILY SERVICE PLAN

Child: Lita Mack **Area:** Communication/Oral Motor

Present Level of Functioning	Outcomes (Who, What Help, Degree of Success)	Intervention/ Strategies/Materials	Timelines/Person Responsible: Initiation	Changed/ Achieved	Review Date/ Comments
Lita imitates some oral movements in play.	For Lita to imitate a variety of facial and mouth movements, with and without sound in play, when modeled, 60% of the time.	Model tongue flapping, lipsmacking, puckering, etc., with and without sound in play. Use mirror -- have Lita look in mirror as you do oral movements.	8/90		
Lita now allows touch on her cheeks without negative reactions.	For Lita to allow her lips and mouth to be touched in play 50% of the time.	Continue to use soft washcloth with pressure on face. Touch objects to lips in play.	8/90		
Lita will take in some food/liquid inconsistently with vomiting decreasing in frequency.	For Lita to continue to take in small amounts of food and liquid when vomiting is less frequent. - decrease Lita's oral sensitivity in order to increase her willingness to accept things orally. - continued encouragement to explore toys orally.	Continue to use soft washcloth with pressure on face. Touch objects to lips in play. Before feeding, use Nuk brush and toothettes orally around gums, lip and mouth area.	8/90		

Date: 9/90
Updates:

INDIVIDUALIZED FAMILY SERVICE PLAN

Child: Lita Mack **Area:** Cognitive

Present Level of Functioning	Outcomes (Who, What Help, Degree of Success)	Intervention/ Strategies/Materials	Timelines/Person Responsible		
			Initiation	Changed/ Achieved	Review Date/ Comments
Lita plays appropriately with just a few toys.	For Lita to play with at least 10 different toys or objects.	Give Lita opportunities to play with a variety of toys, like shape box, jack-in-box, color spin, ball, pop-ups, blocks, musical radio, push and go car, toy piano, musical rhythm instruments. Show her how to play with various toys. Help Lita to play with and operate the toys.	9/90		
Lita's present attention span is 30-60 seconds.	For Lita to play with toys for 3-5 minutes. - For Lita to play appropriately with 50% of toys presented for 2-3 minutes. - For Lita to play with two or three cause and effect toys appropriately for 5 minutes.	Give Lita toys to play with that are appropriate for her developmental level and help her play with them.	9/90		

Date: 9/90
Updates: ______

INDIVIDUALIZED FAMILY SERVICE PLAN

Child: Lita Mack **Area:** Motor

Present Level of Functioning	Outcomes (Who, What Help, Degree of Success)	Intervention/ Strategies/Materials	Timelines/Person Responsible		
			Initiation	Changed/ Achieved	Review Date/ Comments
Lita uses one hand at a time for fine motor tasks.	For Lita to use both her hands to hold toys and objects.	Provide Lita with toys such as 3 pop beads, 2 handled mirror, large legos, spoon and bowl, etc. Model how to use both hands. Physically help Lita to hold with both hands. Fade assistance. Reinforce for attempts to complete task.	9/90		
Lita is beginning to move her arms as if to catch herself when she is tipped to the side from sitting.	For Lita to catch herself with her arms in all directions (to the sides and backward) when tipped in a sitting position.	Give Lita minimal support during balancing activities such as sitting on a small chair or ball. Help Lita sit up from lying on her back (offer her one hand, while she rolls to the side and pushes up with the other).	9/90		

Date: 9/90
Updates:

INDIVIDUALIZED FAMILY SERVICE PLAN

Child: Lita Mack **Area:** Motor (continued)

Present Level of Functioning	Outcomes (Who, What Help, Degree of Success)	Intervention/ Strategies/Materials	Timelines/Person Responsible: Initiation	Changed/ Achieved	Review Date/ Comments
Lita is trying to walk short distances with help from adults.	For Lita to take 5-10 steps independently.	Discuss with Dee and Mark the rooms that Lita is in most often. Discuss ways to change Lita's environment to make space for her to walk by cruising around furniture for support and space for independent walking without having to overcome obstacles in her path. Encourage independent walking by putting reinforcing objects several steps away from Lita or by standing several steps away from her and clapping and talking to her so that she will want to come. Hold arms out for Lita to walk toward adults or objects she wants. Reinforce all of Lita's attempts to walk.	9/90		

TRANSITION PLAN FORM FOR IFSP

Date	Plan of Operation	Who's Responsible	Timeline	Date Achieved
** 12/1/89	Lita will be turning three next October -- ** A transition plan will be initiated 6 months before her third birthday.	Care Coordinator/ Family	Develop plan by March, 1990	
3/1/90	1) Meet with family. Discuss parental rights, get permission to exchange information with the school district, and discuss possible program options.	Care Coordinator	March 1, 1990	
	2) Notify school district. Send pertinent records with written notification. Invite them to transition conference.	Care Coordinator Family	March 2, 1990	
	3) Hold transition conference with family and school district. Develop transition plan. Describe programs and what will happen before enrollment.	Care Coordinator Family School District	March 10, 1990	
	4) Make appointments to visit two possible school sites.	Family	March 20, 1990	
	5) Observe classrooms and talk to teachers.	Family	April, 1990	
	6) List pros and cons of each site.	Family	April, 1990	
	7) Choose best program with input from professionals involved.	Family	May, 1990	
	8) Invite teacher to home. Visit home to observe home interventionist and child during programming.	Family Teacher	May, 1990 May, 1990	
	9) Visit home again to evaluate child.	Teacher	May, 1990	

TRANSITION PLAN FORM FOR IFSP

Date	Plan of Operation	Who's Responsible	Timeline	Date Achieved
	10) Write evaluation report for M-team. M-team scheduled.	Teacher/School District	June 1990	
	11) Hold M-team transition meeting. Offer placement.	Family, Family Advocate (optional) Teacher, School District, Care Coordinator, other professionals.	September 1990	
	12) Sign consent to place if in agreement.	Parents	During M-team September 1990	
	13) Make follow-up call.	Care Coordinator	One Month after child enters school.	
	14) Send written evaluation questionnaire to school district and to parents to evaluate transition.	Care Coordinator	Two months after child enters school.	

TRANSITION PLAN RECORD

Child: Lita **Family:** Dee, Mark, Lita, Jeremy **Date:** January 1991

Sending Agency: LIFT **Receiving Agency:** Lodi School District

	Transition Event	Who	Where/How	Dates
1)	Parents Informed	Care Coordinator	Written Guidelines and Common Problems	
2)	Receiving Agency Notified	Parents/Care Coordinator	Written Notice	
3)	Transfer of Records	Receiving and Sending Agencies/Parents	Written	
4)	Transition Conference	Parents/Sending and Receiving Agencies	Written Plan with Events and Timelines/Written Consent	
5)	Written Transition Plan Developed	Parents/Sending and Receiving Agencies	Sending Agency	
6)	Parents Observe Receiving Agency	Parents/Care Coordinator/ Receiving Teacher		
7)	Receiving Agency Visits Child to Observe and Gather Data for Transition	Receiving Teacher/Child/ Sending Agency		
8)	Transition Meeting -- M-Team	Parents/Sending and Receiving Agencies	Receiving Agency	
9)	Placement	Child/Receiving Agency	Bus Pick Up Schedule/Bus Drop Off	
10)	Follow-Up	Sending and Receiving Agencies	Telephone/Observation/ Visitation	
11)	Transition Evaluation	Parents/Receiving Agency	Written	

Appendix B:
Family-Centered Principles, Guidelines, and Checklists

Guidelines for Enabling and Empowering Families

- Be both positive and proactive in interactions with families.
- Offer help in response to family-identified needs.
- Permit the family to decide whether to accept or reject help.
- Offer help that is normative.
- Offer help that is congruent with the family's appraisal of their needs.
- Promote acceptance of help by keeping the response costs low.
- Permit help to be reciprocated.
- Promote the family's immediate success in mobilizing resources.
- Promote the use of informal support as the principle way of meeting needs.
- Promote a sense of cooperation and joint responsibility for meeting family needs.
- Promote the family member's acquisition of effective behavior for meeting needs.
- Promote the family member's ability to see themselves as an active agent responsible for behavior change.

Source: Dunst, C. J., Trivette, C. M., & Deal, A. G. (1988). *Enabling and empowering families: Principles and guidelines for practice*. Cambridge, MA: Brookline.

Key Elements of Family-Centered Care

- Recognizing that the family is the constant in a child's life, while the service systems and personnel within those systems fluctuate.

- Facilitating parent/professional collaboration at all levels of health care:

  — care of an individual child;
  — program development, implementation, and evaluation; and
  — policy formation.

- Honoring the racial, ethnic, cultural, and socioeconomic diversity of families.

- Recognizing family strengths and individuality and respecting different methods of coping.

- Sharing with parents, on a continuing basis and in a supportive manner, complete and unbiased information.

- Encouraging and facilitating family-to-family support and networking.

- Understanding and incorporating the developmental needs of infants, children, and adolescents and their families into health care systems.

- Implementating comprehensive policies and programs that provide emotional and financial support to meet the needs of families.

- Designing accessible health care systems that are flexible, culturally competent, and responsive to family-identified needs.

Source: National Center for Family-Centered Care. (1990). *What is family-centered care?* (brochure). Bethesda, MD: Association for the Care of Children's Health.

Statement in Support of Families and Their Children

Whereas all children, regardless of disability, belong with families and need enduring relationships with adults, and states and agencies have traditionally not supported the role of families in caring for children with developmental disabilities; therefore, these principles should guide public policy toward families of children with developmental disabilities . . . and the actions of states and agencies when they become involved with families:

1. Every child should have the right to a permanent home and a stable relationship with one or more adults.

2. Families should receive the supports necesssary to maintain their children at home.

3. Family supports should build on existing social networks and natural sources of support.

4. Family supports should maximize the family's control over the services and supports they receive.

5. Family supports should support the entire family.

6. Family support services should encourage the integration of children with disabilities into the community.

7. When children cannot remain with their families for whatever reason, out-of-home placement should be viewed initially as a temporary arrangement and efforts should be directed toward reuniting the family.

8. When families cannot be reunited and when active parental involvement is absent, adoption should be aggressively pursued.

9. While a preferred alternative to any group setting or out-of-home placement, foster care should only be pursued when children cannot live with their families or with adoptive families.

Source: Center on Human Policy. (1986). Syracuse University.

Major Categories of Family Support Principles

Category	Characteristics
Enhancing a Sense of Community	Promoting the coming together of people around shared values and common needs
Mobilizing Resources and Supports	Building support systems that enhance the flow of resources in ways that assist families with parenting responsibilities.
Shared Responsibility and Collaboration	Sharing of ideas and skills by parents and professionals in ways that build and strengthen collaborative arrangements.
Protecting Family Integrity	Protecting the family and its members from abuse and intrusion upon its beliefs and values.
Strengthening Family Functioning	Promoting the capabilities and competencies of families in ways that have empowering consequences.
Proactive Human Service Practices	Adoption of human service-delivery models and practices that support and strengthen family functioning.

Source: Dunst, C. J. (1990, July). *Supporting families: Understanding how they work.* Presentation at the Fifth Annual Early Intervention Summer Institute, Williamsburg, VA.

Checklist for Promoting Shared Responsibility and Collaboration

Policies and practices are valued that encourage partnerships and collaboration between families and both policy makers and practitioners, especially those that involve full disclosure of all pertinent information to families that permits them to make informed decisions. Policies and practices are also valued when they encourage families to be "treated as equals" in all aspects of needs identification and resource mobilization.

- ☐ Does the policy or practice presume that the family and individual family members are competent, as well as have the capacity to become more competent, in mastering a broad range of functions and tasks for meeting needs and mobilizing resources?

- ☐ Does the policy or practice encourage professionals to assume a variety of nontraditional roles and functions that enhance increased collaboration between famillies and professionals?

- ☐ Does the policy or practice promote the use of partnerships between families and professionals as the primary context for identifying needs, mobilizing resources, and strengthening family functioning?

- ☐ Does the policy or practice encourage give-and-take (reciprocity) between families and professionals with regard to the exchange of information, skills, ideas, etc. for meeting needs and mobilizing resources.

- ☐ Does the policy or practice promote the mutual trust, honesty, respect, and open communication between family and professionals as part of collaborative endeavors?

Source: Dunst, C.J. (1990). Family support principles: Checklists for program builders and practitioners. *Family Systems Monograph, 2,* Number 5. Morganton, NC: Family, Infant and Preschool, Western Carolina Center.

Appendix C: Assessment Resources

We Altered Our Process

	Our Old Way		*Our New Way*
1.	Each staff plans his/her own assessment by developmental area.	1.	Planning the assessment.
		a.	The facilitator asks the parents for priorities/questions they wish to have addressed.
		b.	The facilitator then shares this with other team members who help plan a comprehensive assessment that focuses on issues raised by parents.
2.	Each staff conducts his/her own assessments, if possible at a time when a parent can be present so that each assessment can be discussed with the parent. This usually means 3-5 assessment sessions.	2.	The assessment is scheduled when parents can be present; only the facilitator and parent interact with the child while other staff on the team observe and record.
3.	Each staff summarizes his/her assessment findings and recommends goals and treatment settings at a meeting of staff. These staff recommendations are shared with parents at the planning conference.	3.	Immediately after the assessment, the parents share what they have seen during the assessment -- their child's strengths, interests, motivators, problems, and frustrations. Staff supplement these observations as needed to produce a complete description of the child.
4.	Parents are asked if they agree with the recommended goals or have other goals. Staff share their recommended setting(s).	4.	Next, parents draw conclusions or state what seems most important to them regarding the child and define major goals. Again, staff supplement as needed.
5.	To carry out the goals, a primary service setting is chosen by the team. (Generally either home-based for infants and toddlers and center-based for preschoolers).	5.	To carry out the goals, strategies are created that draw upon adults and other children the child encounters throughout the day. Contact with non-delayed peers is a priority.
6.	Each staff provides direct service or consults in his/her area of development as needed and plans the center-based services. Parents reinforce goals in activities at home.	6.	The facilitator consults with family and community resources to carry out the plan and provides direct service only when it cannot be accomplished through consultation. The other staff remain accountable for their area of expertise through active consultation with the facilitator.

7.	The IFSP is reviewed and revised semi-annually; reassessment occurs annually.	7.	The IFSP is reviewed and revised monthly; reassessment and planning occur every four to six months.
8.	Success is measured by: - child progress	8.	Success is measured by: - child progress - parent satisfaction - integrated versus segregated service settings and contact with non-delayed peers - parents' gains in knowledge, skill and confidence in describing their child, setting goals, carrying out strategies, and getting others to carry out strategies
Source: *Kjerland, L. (1986). Early intervention tailor made. Eagan, MN: Project Dakota, Inc.*			

Pre-Assessment Planning With Families

To help a family prepare for assessment, one member of the staff discusses the following information with the family during a pre-assessment visit. The family and the staff member discuss the assessment process, the family's options for participation, and any other information the family may need to prepare for the assessment. The following checklist contains information that should be gathered from or shared with the family before the assessment. This form is not intended to be given a family. Rather, it is a guide for staff members to ensure that families and staff have the information they need to plan an assessment.

Preparing for the Process

An assessment helps us find out the kinds of things your child is doing right now. A number of people come together with your family to form an assessment team. The assessment team observes how your child plays with people and toys.

An assessment usually lasts about 45 minutes to an hour. After the assessment, the team gets together to talk about what everyone saw your child do. During this discussion, called the staffing, your family decides if you want your child and family to participate in our early intervention program. If you do decide that you want the program to be involved with your family, the next step is for you to talk about and decide what kinds of things you want your child to learn. A case manager, who will work closely with you, also is chosen at the staffing.

During the assessment, your family and the other members of the assessment team look at the way your child plays, the way she moves her big and little muscles, the sounds she makes or the words she uses, and the things your child seems to understand. If your family has questions or concerns about your child's eating or drinking, we can look at that, also.

One person, called the assessment facilitator, asks your family questions about what your child does and how he does it. The facilitator's job is to help the assessment go smoothly for you and your child. The facilitator may play with your child or ask you to play with him so that the assessment team has a chance to see the kinds of things your child can do.

You, your child, the facilitator, and any other family members that are participating all sit together on the floor during the assessment so that your child has room to play. Everyone should wear comfortable clothes. There will be toys for your child to play with.

Project Trans/Team, Child Development Resources, 1989

The other members of the team sit on the floor nearby, so that they can observe what your child is doing and hear what you and the facilitator are saying. They usually take notes so that they can remember what they see and hear.

Some of the things the facilitator asks your child to do will be easy, and some things will be very difficult. Your child is not expected to be able to do everything. We hope to see the kinds of things he usually does.

During the assessment, your family and the facilitator may stop playing with your child and just sit back and watch what she does with different toys.

Since family members are part of the team, we hope that you will take an active role in the assessment. You can sit next to your child, comfort or praise him, make suggestions, show the facilitator how to do an activity, or share information about your child. Because you know your child better than anyone else, the information you have to share is very important.

Your child will be in a new place, with people she doesn't know, so she may not do the same things she usually does with you at home. If this happens, don't worry about it. There is plenty of time for you to tell the other team members about what your child does at home, and there will be other times when the rest of the team can see the things your she can do.

We have a form, the *Pre-Assessment Family Questionnaire*, that can help you gather information about your child to share during the assessment and organize your thoughts and questions about the assessment ahead of time. Your family can fill out the form directly, or we can talk about it instead.

What to Bring to the Assessment

On the day of the assessment, you may want to bring things to make your child comfortable. You can bring a bottle or snack, a change of clothes, extra diapers, or a favorite toy. If you have questions or concerns about your child's eating and drinking, bring things to eat or drink that he really likes.

Pre-Assessment Planning With Families
page three

Anyone in your family that you want to participate can come to the assessment, and you can also bring a neighbor or friend with you for support. There may be other professionals who work with your child and family, such as your pediatrician, that you want to invite. Please let us know in advance who will be coming so that we can plan for enough space.

Please bring any medical reports, evaluations, or other papers that you want to share with the rest of the team. If you have filled out the *Pre-Assessment Family Questionnaire*, please bring it with you, along with any notes you may have written down as you prepared for the assessment.

Arrangements

What is a good day and time for your family for the assessment?

The name of your contact person at our program is ___________.
Our phone number and address are

____

____

Please call us if you have any questions and concerns.

Do you have transportation to the assessment? If you have a problem finding transportation, please let us know, and we will help you arrange some.

Do you need any help making child care arrangements for your other children?

Brass Tacks

		Never		Sometimes		Always
1.	Do you conduct assessments at times that are convenient for families? Do you offer choices of times to parents?	1	2	3	4	5
2.	Do you offer parents the option of conducting at least a portion of their children's assessments in their own homes?	1	2	3	4	5
3.	Do you conduct observations of children in natural settings (i.e., home, daycare, classroom) as part of your assessment information?	1	2	3	4	5
4.	Do you ask parents which professionals (disciplines) they want involved in the assessment of their children and do you honor their decisions?	1	2	3	4	5
5.	Do you tell parents they may have anyone else they want present for, or involved in, the assessment(s) of their children (e.g., siblings, grandparents, friends, babysitters, professionals from other agencies)?	1	2	3	4	5
6.	Do you offer parents choices regarding the assessment tools/measures that will be used for their child and the methods used for administration?	1	2	3	4	5
7.	Do you offer parents a range of options for how they can be involved in the assessment of their children? Do you honor their decisions regarding the level or type of involvement they prefer?	1	2	3	4	5
8.	Do you reveal and explain assessment results to parents immediately after they are obtained (i.e., on the same day)?	1	2	3	4	5
9.	Do you offer parents a clear choice as to who assessment information will be shared with and how this will be done?	1	2	3	4	5
10.	Do you discuss assessment results using terms that are readily understood and meaningful to parents?	1	2	3	4	5
11.	Do you write children's assessment reports in such a way as to reflect the parents' priorities?	1	2	3	4	5
12.	Do you write reports in a way that is readily understood and meaningful to parents?	1	2	3	4	5
13.	Do you give a copy of (the) assessment report(s) to parents?	1	2	3	4	5
14.	Do you offer parents the opportunity to write a portion of the assessment report(s), sign the report(s), or make suggestions for changes before a final copy is filed or sent out?	1	2	3	4	5
15.	Do you clearly offer parents the opportunity for parents to be present at all discussions regarding the planning of the child's assessment or discussing the results of the child's assessment?	1	2	3	4	5
16.	Do you only write recommendations in your assessment reports if they have been discussed with and agreed upon by parents?	1	2	3	4	5

Source: McWilliam, P. J., & Winton, P. J. (1990). *Brass Tacks*. Chapel Hill, NC: Frank Porter Graham Child Development Center, University of North Carolina, Chapel Hill.

Appendix D
Resources for Identifying Family Concerns, Priorities, and Resources

Exercise: Social Support

1. Who are the members of my family?

2. What other relatives, close friends, neighbors, co-workers, church or synagogue members, and others provide me with social support?

3. What roadblocks do I have to using friends, neighbors and relatives for social support? It may be helpful to divide those roadblocks into two groups; those that are practical roadblocks, such as lack of time or transportation, and those that are value roadblocks, such as believing you have sole responsibility, or that you do not want to burden others.

   Practical Roadblocks

   Value Roadblocks

4. What steps could I use to overcome one of these roadblocks?

   Practical Roadblocks

   Value Roadblock

   Steps

   Steps

Source: Summers, J.A., Turnbull, A.P., & Brotherson, M.J. (December, 1985). *Coping strategies for families with disabled children.*

5. Listed below are several kinds of people who might make up your social support network, along with a scale to rate how helpful they are. Circle the number that best describes how helpful each one is to you. Leave blank if that person or persons does not apply to you. Use a different color pen or crayon for each family member who fills this out, and compare your answers.

	Not at All Helpful	Sometimes Helpful	Generally Helpful	Very Helpful	Extremely Helpful
1. My parents	0	1	2	3	4
2. My spouse's parents	0	1	2	3	4
3. My relatives/kin	0	1	2	3	4
4. My spouse's relatives/kin	0	1	2	3	4
5. Husband or wife	0	1	2	3	4
6. My friends	0	1	2	3	4
7. My spouse's friends	0	1	2	3	4
8. My own children	0	1	2	3	4
9. Other parents	0	1	2	3	4
10. My family physician	0	1	2	3	4
11. Co-workers	0	1	2	3	4
12. Parent, spouse, or other self-help groups	0	1	2	3	4
13. School (teachers, therapists, psychologists, etc,)	0	1	2	3	4
14. Professional agencies (public health, social services, respite care, activity programs)	0	1	2	3	4
15. Civic groups/clubs	0	1	2	3	4
16. Clergy and congregation of your place of worship	0	1	2	3	4

This questionnaire was adapted, with permission, from a survey prepared by Marie Bristol, Frank Porter Graham Child Development Center, University of North Carolina at Chapel Hill, 1983.

Family Needs Survey

(Revised, 1990b)

Child's Name:________________________ Person Completing Survey:________________

Date Completed:_____/____/_____ Relationship to Child: ____________________

Dear Parent:

Many families of young children have needs for information or support. If you wish, our staff are very willing to discuss these needs with you and work with you to identify resources that might be helpful.

Listed below are some needs commonly expressed by families. It would be helpful to us if you would check in the columns on the right any topics you would like to discuss. At the end there is a place for you to describe other topics not included in the list.

If you choose to complete this form, the information you provide will be kept confidential. If you would prefer not to complete the survey at this time, you may keep it for your records.

Would you like to discuss this topic with a staff person from our program?

TOPICS	No	Not Sure	Yes
Information			
1. How children grow and develop			
2. How to play or talk with my child			
3. How to teach my child			
4. How to handle my child's behavior			
5. Information about any condition or disability my child might have			
6. Information about services that are presently available for my child			
7. Information about the services my child might receive in the future			
Family & Social Support			
1. Talking with someone in my family about concerns			
2. Having friends to talk to			
3. Finding more time for myself			
4. Helping my spouse accept any condition our child might have			
5. Helping our family discuss problems and reach solutions			
6. Helping our family support each other during difficult times			
7. Deciding who will do household chores, child care, and other family tasks			
8. Deciding on and doing family recreational activities			
Financial			
1. Paying for expenses such as food, housing, medical care, clothing, or transportation			
2. Getting any special equipment my child needs			
3. Paying for therapy, day care, or other services my child needs			
4. Counseling or help in getting a job			
5. Paying for babysitting or respite care			
6. Paying for toys that my child needs			

Would you like to discuss this topic with a staff person from our program?

TOPICS	No	Not Sure	Yes
Explaining to Others			
1. Explaining my child's condition to my parents or my spouse's parents			
2. Explaining my child's condition to his or her siblings			
3. Knowing how to respond when friends, neighbors, or strangers ask questions about my child			
4. Explaining my child's condition to other children			
5. Finding reading material about other families who have a child like mine			
Child Care			
1. Locating babysitters or respite care providers who are willing and able to care for my child.			
2. Locating a day care program or preschool for my child			
3. Getting appropriate care for my child in a church or synagogue during religious services			
Professional Support			
1. Meeting with a minister, priest, or rabbi			
2. Meeting with a counselor (psychologist, social worker, psychiatrist)			
3. More time to talk to my child's teacher or therapist			
Community Services			
1. Meeting & talking with other parents who have a child like mine			
2. Locating a doctor who understands me and my child's needs			
3. Locating a dentist who will see my child			

Other: Please list other topics or provide any other information that you feel would be helpful to discuss.

____

____

Is there a particular person with whom you would prefer to meet?

____

____

Thank you for your time.
We hope this form will be helpful to you in identifying the services that you feel are important.

Family Support Scale

Carl J. Dunst, Vicki Jenkins, & Carol M. Trivette

Name: ______________________________ **Date:** ________________

Listed below are people and groups that oftentimes are helpful to members of a family raising a young child. This questionnaire asks you to indicate how helpful each source is to **your family.**

Please **circle** the response that best describes how helpful the sources have been to your family during the past **3 to 6 months**. If a source of help has not been available to your family during this period of time, circle the NA (Not Available) response.

How helpful has each of the following been to you in terms of raising your child(ren):	Not Available	Not at All Helpful	Sometimes Helpful	Generally Helpful	Very Helpful	Extremely Helpful
1. My parents	NA	1	2	3	4	5
2. My spouse or partner's parents	NA	1	2	3	4	5
3. My relatives/kin	NA	1	2	3	4	5
4. My spouse or partner's relatives/kin	NA	1	2	3	4	5
5. Spouse or partner	NA	1	2	3	4	5
6. My friends	NA	1	2	3	4	5
7. My spouse or partner's friends	NA	1	2	3	4	5
8. My own children	NA	1	2	3	4	5
9. Other parents	NA	1	2	3	4	5
10. Co-workers	NA	1	2	3	4	5
11. Parent groups	NA	1	2	3	4	5
12. Social groups/clubs	NA	1	2	3	4	5
13. Church members/minister	NA	1	2	3	4	5
14. My family or child's physician	NA	1	2	3	4	5
15. Early childhood intervention program	NA	1	2	3	4	5
16. School/day-care center	NA	1	2	3	4	5
17. Professional helpers (social workers, therapists, teachers, etc.)	NA	1	2	3	4	5
18. Professional agencies (public health, social services, mental health, etc.)	NA	1	2	3	4	5
19. ______________________	NA	1	2	3	4	5
20. ______________________	NA	1	2	3	4	5

Source: C.J. Dunst, C.M. Trivette, and A.G. Deal (1988). *Enabling and empowering families: Principles and guidelines for practice.* Cambridge, MA: Brookline Books. May be reproduced.

Family Needs Scale

Carl J. Dunst, Carolyn S. Cooper, Janet C. Weeldreyer, Kathy D. Snyder, & Joyce H. Chase

Name ______________________________ Date ______________

This scale asks you to indicate if you have a need for any type of help or assistance in 41 different areas. Please *circle* the response that best describes how you feel about needing help in those areas.

To what extent do you feel the need for any of the following types of help or assistance:	Not Applicable	Almost Never	Seldom	Sometimes	Often	Almost Always
1. Having money to buy necessities and pay bills	NA	1	2	3	4	5
2. Budgeting money	NA	1	2	3	4	5
3. Paying for special needs of my child	NA	1	2	3	4	5
4. Saving money for the future	NA	1	2	3	4	5
5. Having clean water to drink	NA	1	2	3	4	5
6. Having food for two meals for my family	NA	1	2	3	4	5
7. Having time to cook healthy meals for my family	NA	1	2	3	4	5
8. Feeding my child	NA	1	2	3	4	5
9. Getting a place to live	NA	1	2	3	4	5
10. Having plumbing, lighting, heat	NA	1	2	3	4	5
11. Getting furniture, clothes, toys	NA	1	2	3	4	5
12. Completing chores, repairs, home improvements	NA	1	2	3	4	5
13. Adapting my house for my child	NA	1	2	3	4	5
14. Getting a job	NA	1	2	3	4	5
15. Having a satisfying job	NA	1	2	3	4	5
16. Planning for future job of my child	NA	1	2	3	4	5
17. Getting where I need to go	NA	1	2	3	4	5
18. Getting in touch with people I need to talk to	NA	1	2	3	4	5
19. Transporting my child	NA	1	2	3	4	5
20. Having special travel equipment for my child	NA	1	2	3	4	5
21. Finding someone to talk to about my child	NA	1	2	3	4	5
22. Having someone to talk to	NA	1	2	3	4	5
23. Having medical and dental care for my family	NA	1	2	3	4	5
24. Having time to take care of myself	NA	1	2	3	4	5
25. Having emergency health care	NA	1	2	3	4	5
26. Finding special dental and medical care for my child	NA	1	2	3	4	5
27. Planning for future health needs	NA	1	2	3	4	5
28. Managing the daily needs of my child at home	NA	1	2	3	4	5
29. Caring for my child during work hours	NA	1	2	3	4	5
30. Having emergency child care	NA	1	2	3	4	5
31. Getting respite care for my child	NA	1	2	3	4	5
32. Finding care for my child in the future	NA	1	2	3	4	5
33. Finding a school placement for my child	NA	1	2	3	4	5
34. Getting equipment or therapy for my child	NA	1	2	3	4	5
35. Having time to take my child to appointments	NA	1	2	3	4	5
36. Exploring future educational options for my child	NA	1	2	3	4	5
37. Expanding my education, skills, and interests	NA	1	2	3	4	5
38. Doing things that I enjoy	NA	1	2	3	4	5
39. Doing things with my family	NA	1	2	3	4	5
40. Participation in parent groups or clubs	NA	1	2	3	4	5
41. Traveling/vacationing with my child	NA	1	2	3	4	5

Source: C.J. Dunst, C.M. Trivette, and A.G. Deal (1988). *Enabling and empowering families: Principles and guidelines for practice.* Cambridge, MA: Brookline Books. May be reproduced.

Parent Needs' Survey

Date: ______________________________

Name of Person Completing Form: ______________________________

Relationship to Child: ______________________________

Parents of young children have many different needs. Not all parents need the same kinds of help. For each of the needs listed below, please check (X) the space that best describes your need or desire for help in that area. Although we may not be able to help you with all your needs, your answers will help us improve our program.

		I really need some help in this area.	**I would like some help, but my need is not that great.**	**I don't need any help in this area.**
1.	More information about my child's disability.			
2.	Someone who can help me feel better about myself.			
3.	Help with child care.			
4.	More money/financial help.			
5.	Someone who can baby sit for a day or evening so I can get away.			
6.	Better medical care for my child.			
7.	More information about child development.			
8.	More information about behavior problems.			
9.	More information about programs that can help my child.			
10.	Counseling to help me cope with my situation.			
11.	Better/more frequent teaching or therapy services for my child.			
12.	Day care so I can get a job.			
13.	A bigger or better house or apartment.			
14.	More information about how I can help my child.			
15.	More information about nutrition or feeding.			
16.	Learning how to handle my other children's jealousy of their brother or sister.			
17.	Problems with in-laws or other relatives.			
18.	Problems with friends or neighbors.			
19.	Special equipment to meet my child's needs.			
20.	More friends who have a child like mine.			
21.	Someone to talk to about my problems.			

(over)

		I really need some help in this area.	I would like some help, but my need is not that great.	I don't need any help in this area.
22.	Problems with my husband (wife).			
23.	A car or other form of transportation.			
24.	Medical care for myself.			
25.	More time for myself.			
26.	More time to be with my child.			
Please list any needs we have forgotten:				
27.				
28.				
29.				
30.				
31.				
32.				
33.				
34.				
35.				

Source: Seligman, M. & Benjamin Darling, R. (1989). *Ordinary families, special children: A systems approach to childhood disability*. New York: Guilford Press.

How Can We Help?

Family Name: ______________________________ **Date:** ________________

All children and families enrolled at CDR have their own strengths and needs. Please use this form to tell us how we can be most helpful to your family. We know that your needs will change from time to time and that this will just be a beginning to help us to plan together with you. Answer only those questions that you think will help us know how we can be most helpful to you and your family.

What pleases you most about your child?

What worries you most about your child?

What kind of help or information do you want from CDR?

Are there things you feel are going well for your family and child right now?

What would you like your child to be able to do in the next several months?

What would you like for your family in the next several months?

Beside your family, are there other people you would like to include in the assessment and planning meeting for your child and family?

Child Development Resources, 4/91

How Can We Help?

Our Family Would Like . . .

	We Have Enough	We Would Like More	Not Sure
Information about:			
child development	______	______	______
child behavior	______	______	______
nutrition/feeding	______	______	______
our child's health problems	______	______	______
our child's developmental problems	______	______	______
toys or books for our child and how to get them	______	______	______
other: ____________________			
Help with child care:			
finding daily child care	______	______	______
finding babysitters or respite care	______	______	______
finding a preschool for our child	______	______	______
teaching care providers how to take care of our child	______	______	______
finding ways to pay for child care	______	______	______
deciding on or evaluating child care settings	______	______	______
other: ____________________			
To know about community services for our child and family:			
GED and other adult education	______	______	______
transportation to CDR services	______	______	______
public transportation	______	______	______
who can help with transportation to doctor's appointments and other special services for our child	______	______	______
food, food stamps, WIC, or other nutrition programs	______	______	______
housing	______	______	______
fuel	______	______	______
clothing	______	______	______
finding a job or job training	______	______	______
financial assistance	______	______	______
individual or family counseling	______	______	______
other: ____________________			

How Can We Help?

	We Have Enough	We Would Like More	Not Sure
To know more about getting medical and dental care for our family:			
finding a doctor or dentist	________	________	________
getting help paying for health care	________	________	________
getting and using special equipment and supplies for our child	________	________	________
training in how to give First Aid/CPR for our family and others	________	________	________
family planning/birth control	________	________	________
other: ________________________			
Help talking about our child:			
to our children, nieces, nephews, and to other children	________	________	________
to our friends and other relatives	________	________	________
to doctors and nurses to get the information and help we want	________	________	________
to people at CDR	________	________	________
to other professionals (social workers, teachers, others) about our baby and ourselves to get the information and help we want	________	________	
to other people we meet	________	________	________
other: ________________________			
Help planning for the future/transition:			
eligibility and the public school	________	________	________
special education process	________	________	________
eligibility, legal rights, parent's role	________	________	________
visiting other service settings	________	________	________
determining the best setting for our child	________	________	________
other: ________________________			

Please tell us the other ways we might be able to help:

CDR provides many services to help you help your baby grow and develop. Families often need many services we cannot provide. When that happens, your service coordinator will help you find out how to get other community services.

Appendix E:
Resources for Evaluating the IFSP Process

Family-Centered Program Rating Scale
Parents' Scale

There are lots of different ways programs can serve families of young children with special needs. We would like to know which ways are important to you and how well you think your program is doing.

Directions: Each statement on this rating scale finishes a sentence which begins with the words at the top of the section. For example, statements in the first section begin with:

IN THIS PROGRAM. . .

All of the statements in the first section finish this sentence. There are four sections; each section has a different beginning. Read each statement and mark it two times:

1. Tell us how well your program is doing on each item. Circle the letters that most closely tell us your opinion about how your program is doing.

   P = Poor

   OK = Okay

   G = Good

   E = Excellent

2. Tell us how important the item is to you, personally. Circle the letters that most closely tell us how important this item is to you.

   NI = Not Important

   SI = Somewhat Important

   I = Important

   VI = Very Important

Start Here

A. IN THIS PROGRAM. . .

1. meetings with my family are scheduled when and where they are most convenient for us.	P OK G E	NI SI I VI
2. the information staff members give my family helps us make decisions about our child.	P OK G E	NI SI I VI
3. someone on the staff can help my family get services from other agencies.	P OK G E	NI SI I VI
4. services can change quickly when my family's or child's needs change.	P OK G E	NI SI I VI

	How well does your program do this? P = Poor OK = Okay G = Good E = Excellent	How important is this to you? NI = Not Important SI = Somewhat Important I = Important VI = Very Important
IN THIS PROGRAM...		
5. services are planned with my family's transportation and scheduling needs in mind.	P OK G E	NI SI I VI
6. someone on the staff can help my family communicate with all the other professionals serving us and our child.	P OK G E	NI SI I VI
7. the program administrator makes my family feel comfortable when we have questions or complaints.	P OK G E	NI SI I VI
8. the IEP, or IFSP (Individualized Family Service Plan), is used as a "plan of action."	P OK G E	NI SI I VI
9. there is a comfortable way to work out disagreements between families and staff members.	P OK G E	NI SI I VI
B. THE PROGRAM...		
10. helps my family when we want information about jobs, money, counseling, housing, or other basic family needs.	P OK G E	NI SI I VI
11. gives the other children in my family support and information about their brother's or sister's disability.	P OK G E	NI SI I VI
12. gives us information on how to meet other families of children with similar needs.	P OK G E	NI SI I VI
13. offers special times for fathers to talk with other fathers and with the staff.	P OK G E	NI SI I VI
14. offers information in a variety of ways (written, videotape, cassette tape, workshop, etc.).	P OK G E	NI SI I VI
15. helps my family expect good things in the future for ourselves and our children.	P OK G E	NI SI I VI
16. coordinates its work with other agencies that my family uses.	P OK G E	NI SI I VI

	How well does your program do this? P = Poor, OK = Okay, G = Good, E = Excellent	How important is this to you? NI = Not Important, SI = Somewhat Important, I = Important, VI = Very Important
C. STAFF MEMBERS...		
17. are available to go to doctors or other service providers with my family to help ask questions, sort out infomation, and decide on services.	P OK G E	NI SI I VI
18. don't talk about or write down my family's private matters.	P OK G E	NI SI I VI
19. help my family learn how to teach our child special skills.	P OK G E	NI SI I VI
20. don't strictly follow checklists or lists of questions when asking about my family's strengths and needs.	P OK G E	NI SI I VI
21. understand that my family balances our child's needs with other family members' needs.	P OK G E	NI SI I VI
22. give information to help my family explain our child's needs to friends and other family members.	P OK G E	NI SI I VI
23. help my family plan for the future.	P OK G E	NI SI I VI
24. don't ask my family about personal matters unless it is necessary.	P OK G E	NI SI I VI
25. respect whatever level of involvement my family chooses in making decisions.	P OK G E	NI SI I VI
26. don't rush my family to make changes until we are ready to.	P OK G E	NI SI I VI
27. help my family feel we can make a positive difference in our child's life.	P OK G E	NI SI I VI
28. give my family time to talk about our experiences and things that are important to us.	P OK G E	NI SI I VI
29. are honest with my family.	P OK G E	NI SI I VI
30. create ways for my family to be involved in making decisions about services.	P OK G E	NI SI I VI

	How well does your program do this? P = Poor, OK = Okay, G = Good, E = Excellent	How important is this to you? NI = Not Important, SI = Somewhat Important, I = Important, VI = Very Important
STAFF MEMBERS...		
31. give my family clear and complete information about our child's disability.	P OK G E	NI SI I VI
32. tell my family what they have learned right after our child's evaluation.	P OK G E	NI SI I VI
33. don't act rushed or in a hurry when they meet with me or my family.	P OK G E	NI SI I VI
34. don't ask my family to repeat information that is already on file.	P OK G E	NI SI I VI
35. don't try to tell my family what we need or don't need.	P OK G E	NI SI I VI
36. help my family feel more confident about working with professionals.	P OK G E	NI SI I VI
37. give clear and complete information about families' rights.	P OK G E	NI SI I VI
38. give my family clear and complete information about available services.	P OK G E	NI SI I VI
39. help my family feel more comfortable when asking for help and support from friends and other family members.	P OK G E	NI SI I VI
40. regularly ask my family about how well the program is doing and what changes we might like to see.	P OK G E	NI SI I VI
41. offer to visit my family in our home.	P OK G E	NI SI I VI
42. offer ideas on how my family can have fun with our children.	P OK G E	NI SI I VI
43. treat my family as the true experts on our child when planning and providing services.	P OK G E	NI SI I VI

STAFF MEMBERS. . .	How well does your program do this? P = Poor, OK = Okay, G = Good, E = Excellent	How important is this to you? NI = Not Important, SI = Somewhat Important, I = Important, VI = Very Important
44. give my family clear and complete explanations about our child.	P OK G E	NI SI I VI
45. help my family learn how to help our children feel good about themselves.	P OK G E	NI SI I VI
46. don't overwhelm us with too much information.	P OK G E	NI SI I VI
47. get to know my family and let us get to know them.	P OK G E	NI SI I VI
48. really listen to my family.	P OK G E	NI SI I VI
49. help my family use problem-solving skills for making decisions about ourselves and our children.	P OK G E	NI SI I VI
50. give information that helps my family with our children's everyday needs (feeding, clothing, playing, health care, safety, friendship, etc.).	P OK G E	NI SI I VI
51. keep policymakers informed about service gaps in the community that keep children from getting needed help.	P OK G E	NI SI I VI
52. help my family see what we are doing well.	P OK G E	NI SI I VI
53. make it easy for parents to meet and visit with each other.	P OK G E	NI SI I VI
54. respect differences among children, families, and families' ways of life.	P OK G E	NI SI I VI
55. ask my family's opinions and include us in the process of evaluating our child.	P OK G E	NI SI I VI
56. are friendly and easy to talk to.	P OK G E	NI SI I VI
57. help my family feel more confident that we are experts on our children.	P OK G E	NI SI I VI
58. enjoy working with my family and child.	P OK G E	NI SI I VI

	How well does your program do this? P = Poor, OK = Okay, G = Good, E = Excellent	How important is this to you? NI = Not Important, SI = Somewhat Important, I = Important, VI = Very Important
STAFF MEMBERS...		
59. don't make insensitive comments about my child or family.	P OK G E	NI SI I VI
60. help my family sort out what things we can and can't control in our child's life.	P OK G E	NI SI I VI
61. help my family feel we are not alone, that there are others who will help us.	P OK G E	NI SI I VI
62. help my family to have a normal life.	P OK G E	NI SI I VI
63. explain how information about my family will be used.	P OK G E	NI SI I VI
64. give my family information about how children usually grow and develop.	P OK G E	NI SI I VI
65. help my family see the good things we are doing to meet our child's needs.	P OK G E	NI SI I VI
66. consider my family's strengths and needs when planning ways to meet our child's needs.	P OK G E	NI SI I VI
D. MY FAMILY...		
67. is included in all meetings about ourselves and our child.	P OK G E	NI SI I VI
68. receives complete copies of all reports about us and our child.	P OK G E	NI SI I VI
69. is encouraged to talk about how we feel about ourselves and our child.	P OK G E	NI SI I VI
70. is an important part of the team when our IEP, or IFSP (Individualized Family Service Plan), is developed, reviewed, or changed.	P OK G E	NI SI I VI

COMMENTS

What things about your child's program make it especially helpful and welcoming to your family?

What are ways in which your child's program could be <u>more</u> helpful and welcoming to your family?

Source: Summers, J. A., Turnbull, A. P., Murphy, D. L., et al. (1991). *Family-centered program rating scale: Parents' scale*. Lawrence, Kansas: Beach Center on Families and Disability, The University of Kansas.

Parent Satisfaction Survey
(Project Dakota Outreach)

Please indicate how satisfied you are with services you receive from your child's program. For each item put a check to show how strongly you agree or disagree with that statement. Your response to <u>each</u> statement is important -- any unanswered items have a negative effect on the final score.

Goal I - Program and Staff Responsiveness	**Strongly Disagree**	**Disagree**	**Agree**	**Strongly Agree**
The staff listen and respond to my concerns, questions, and ideas.	____	____	____	____
In my meetings with staff (for assessments, conferences, monthly updates, etc.), I feel I am an active member of the team and not just a listener.	____	____	____	____
Although one staff member mainly serves my child, I feel that we receive the expertise of other staff.	____	____	____	____
Staff give me information that is clear and useful to me.	____	____	____	____
I feel the program for my child includes what is important to me.	____	____	____	____
My child's program meets my child's needs.	____	____	____	____
The help my child is getting is based on his/her individual needs.	____	____	____	____
I am satisfied with my child's progress since beginning this program.	____	____	____	____
The help I get fits into our family routines and activities.	____	____	____	____
The staff respect the limits my family puts on our time and energy for our child's program.	____	____	____	____
I am informed of a variety of choices for how my child could be served.	____	____	____	____

Goal II - Growth in Knowledge and Skills for Helping Your Child

Because of my participation with the program....	Strongly Disagree	Disagree	Agree	Strongly Agree
I am more able to look at my child and see what he/she is learning to do.	____	____	____	____
I have learned about helping my child.	____	____	____	____
I enjoy my child more.	____	____	____	____
I know what my child needs to learn.	____	____	____	____
I am aware of how ordinary activities are part of my child's learning and development.	____	____	____	____
I feel more confident about how my family and I are helping our child.	____	____	____	____
I am more aware of how to help my child's development.	____	____	____	____
I have a clearer picture of my child's special needs at this time.	____	____	____	____
I feel satisfied that my child's strengths are being discussed.	____	____	____	____
I know more about how to set goals and strategies for my child.	____	____	____	____

Comments: (Please comment if you've checked any items "Strongly Disagree" or "Disagree.")

____

____

____

____

Goal III - Growth in Understanding Normal Behavior and Problems

Because of my participation with the program....	Strongly Disagree	Disagree	Agree	Strongly Agree
I more strongly value my child spending time with children who don't have developmental delays.	____	____	____	____
I am more aware of how my child is like other children.	____	____	____	____
I know more ways to get my child to cooperate.	____	____	____	____
I am getting the help I need to learn about handling my child's behavior.	____	____	____	____

Comments: (Please comment if you've checked any items "Strongly Disagree" or "Disagree.")

____

____

Goal IV - Utilization of Community Resources

Because of my participation with the program....	Strongly Disagree	Disagree	Agree	Strongly Agree
I know more about community agencies, services, and programs that can help my child or my family.	____	____	____	____
I get help from staff when I want other programs or people to work with me, my child, or my family.	____	____	____	____
I now have contact with services and programs in the community who may help my child or my family.	____	____	____	____
I am satisfied with the communication between my child's team and community resource persons involved in my child's program.	____	____	____	____
I am able to get information that is important to the health and happiness of my family and child.	____	____	____	____

Comments: (Please comment if you've checked any items "Strongly Disagree" or "Disagree.")

____

____

Goal V - Building a Support System

Because of my participation with the program....	**Strongly Disagree**	**Disagree**	**Agree**	**Strongly Agree**
My partner/my family are more involved in my child's learning.	____	____	____	____
I have more friends or other children helping me help my child.	____	____	____	____
Staff helped the people I know be more caring and understanding of my child.	____	____	____	____
Staff helped me get to know other people who are caring and understanding.	____	____	____	____
I have gotten support from other parents.	____	____	____	____
I feel less alone as the parent of my child.	____	____	____	____
Staff are willing and able to help my family and friends when we have concerns or questions about my child.	____	____	____	____

Comments: (Please comment if you've checked any items "Strongly Disagree" or "Disagree.")

____

____

My child is _____ years ____ months old.

Signature (optional) ____

THANK YOU FOR GIVING US THIS FEEDBACK!

Source: Project Dakota, 1987.

Evaluation of Team Effort to Develop and Provide Services and Support

By IFSP Team Members as Team Evaluation or Self-Evaluation.

Can be used at any time throughout or after the process.

What worked well?	How could the team be more responsive, effective, or supportive?
What needs to be improved?	Family satisfaction with services.

Source: Minnesota Individual Family Service Plan (draft). Minnesota Department of Health, 1991.

Appendix F:
User's Reactions to Monograph

Reaction Sheet

NEC*TAS and ACCH are very interested in knowing the reaction of professionals and families to the content and format of the monograph. We sincerely ask that anyone using the monograph take the time to complete this brief reaction sheet. For more extensive comments, we encourage you to attach extra pages for your comments. If more than one person is using the same monograph, please take a moment to duplicate the reaction sheet for all monograph users so that we can obtain the greatest possible number of reactions. Please return completed reaction sheets to:

Association for the Care of Children's Health
7910 Woodmont Avenue, Suite 300
Bethesda, MD 20814

Reactions to Monograph Structure

1. How would you rate the overall structure of the monograph? *(circle one)* 1 2 3 4
   Poor Excellent

2. How would you describe the overall length of the mongraph?
   - ☐ Just right
   - ☐ Too long If so, what content should be shortened?________________
   - ☐ Too short If so, what content should be added?________________

3. How would you rate the overall writing style of the monograph? *(circle one)* 1 2 3 4
   Poor Excellent

4. How would you describe the use of references in the monograph? *(circle one)* 1 2 3 4
   Poor Excellent

Reactions to Content -- Chapters

1. Overview
- Useful? ☐ Yes ☐ No
  If no, suggestions? ____________
- Complete? ☐ Yes ☐ No
  If no, suggestions? ____________

2. Philosophy and Conceptual Framework
- Useful? ☐ Yes ☐ No
  If no, suggestions? ____________
- Complete? ☐ Yes ☐ No
  If no, suggestions? ____________

3. IFSP Sequence
- Useful? ☐ Yes ☐ No
  If no, suggestions? ____________
- Complete? ☐ Yes ☐ No
  If no, suggestions? ____________

4. Building Positive Relationships
- Useful? ☐ Yes ☐ No
  If no, suggestions? ____________
- Complete? ☐ Yes ☐ No
  If no, suggestions? ____________

5. Identifying Children's Strengths and Needs
- Useful? ☐ Yes ☐ No
  If no, suggestions? ____________
- Complete? ☐ Yes ☐ No
  If no, suggestions? ____________

6. Family Concerns, Priorities, and Resources
- Useful? ☐ Yes ☐ No
  If no, suggestions? ____________
- Complete? ☐ Yes ☐ No
  If no, suggestions? ____________

7. Developing the IFSP
- Useful? ☐ Yes ☐ No
  If no, suggestions? ____________
- Complete? ☐ Yes ☐ No
  If no, suggestions? ____________

8. Implementation of the IFSP
- Useful? ☐ Yes ☐ No
  If no, suggestions? ____________
- Complete? ☐ Yes ☐ No
  If no, suggestions? ____________

9. **Future Directions**
- Useful? ☐ Yes ☐ No
  If no, suggestions? ____________________
- Complete? ☐ Yes ☐ No
  If no, suggestions? ____________________

Reactions to Content -- Appendices

Sample IFSPs
- Useful? ☐ Yes ☐ No
  If no, suggestions? ____________________
- Complete? ☐ Yes ☐ No
  If no, suggestions? ____________________

Family-Centered Principles, Guidelines, and Checklists
- Useful? ☐ Yes ☐ No
  If no, suggestions? ____________________
- Complete? ☐ Yes ☐ No
  If no, suggestions? ____________________

Assessment Resources
- Useful? ☐ Yes ☐ No
  If no, suggestions? ____________________
- Complete? ☐ Yes ☐ No
  If no, suggestions? ____________________

Resources for Identifying Family Concerns, Priorities, and Resources
- Useful? ☐ Yes ☐ No
  If no, suggestions? ____________________
- Complete? ☐ Yes ☐ No
  If no, suggestions? ____________________

Resources for Evaluating the IFSP Process
- Useful? ☐ Yes ☐ No
  If no, suggestions? ____________________
- Complete? ☐ Yes ☐ No
  If no, suggestions? ____________________

Overall Reactions

1. Do you feel this monograph is worth its cost?
   ☐ Yes ☐ No

2. Would you recommend the use of this monograph to others?
   ☐ Yes ☐ No

3. Do you have any general reactions to the monograph that you would like to share?

   ____

   ____

   ____

Information About You

1. How did you obtain this monograph? *(circle one)*
   I ordered it   It was sent to me unrequested
   It was loaned to me

2. How will you use this monograph? *(circle one)*
   Personal reference   For training parents
   For training professionals

   If you will use this monograph to train others, are you on the faculty of a college or unversity training program? ☐ Yes ☐ No

3. Are you a parent of a child with special needs?
   ☐ Yes ☐ No

4. Are you a professional providing early intervention services to children and families?
   ☐ Yes ☐ No

5. Are you a student preparing to provide early intervention services to children and families?
   ☐ Yes ☐ No

6. What title best describes your discipline? *(circle one)*
   Early Intervention   Social Work   Medicine
   Special Education   Speech/Language Therapy
   Physical or Occupational Therapy   Nursing
   Psychology   Child Life
   Other (describe) ______________

Thank you for sharing your reactions.